Gospeltelling

to a

Digital Culture

The Forensic Reconstruction
of a Good Story

D. Jonathan Watts

Wyndham Hall Press
Lima, Oh.

Gospeltelling to a Digital Culture
The Forensic Reconstruction of a Good Story

D. Jonathan Watts

Published by
Wyndham Hall Press
5050 Kerr Rd
Lima, OH 45806

www.wyndhamhallpress.com

Library of Congress Cataloging-in-Publication Data
Watts, D. Jonathan.
Gospeltelling to a digital culture : the forensic reconstruction
of a good story / D. Jonathan Watts.
p. cm.
Includes bibliographical references.
ISBN-13: 978-1-55605-404-4 (pbk.)
ISBN-10: 1-55605-404-1 (pbk.)
1. Preaching. 2. Storytelling--Religious aspects--Christianity. 3. Public
worship. I. Title. II. Title: Gospel telling to a digital culture.
BV4211.3.W38 2007
251--dc22

Printed in the United States of America

I Dedicate This Work

In memory of my father, David L. Watts, who told me my first stories, who gave me my first homiletics lesson while sitting on a porch during a family vacation, and whose words of wisdom I still hold dear.

In honor of my wife, Karen Y. Watts, who has been more than patient with this wandering soul.

CONTENTS

Not all who wander are lost.
~J.R.R. Tolkien

ACKNOWLEDGEMENTS

I would like to express my appreciation to those who have encouraged me in my wanderings:

Dr. Thomas E. Boomershine, a friend and mentor, for his patience and guidance as I have wandered through the fields of oral tradition.

Dr. Leonard I. Sweet, for his futuristic vision and his faith in my work and dreams.

Dr. John Morgan and the Staff of The Graduate Theological Foundation for their support and encouragement.

INTRODUCTION

Surrounded by the gray-tone concrete walls of Canon Chapel at Emory University, the great composer/conductor Robert Shaw spoke one morning, permeating the atmosphere with the fragrance of his life. I sat in awe of the legend, hanging on to his every word. The homily was based on the opening text of John's Gospel, "In the beginning was the Word, and the Word was with God and the Word was God." Of all the images he rained down upon us that day, one in particular has haunted me because of its truth. Shaw said, "Two thousand years ago the Word became Flesh. And, for the past two thousand years, humanity has been trying to turn the Flesh back into just a word."

During my tenure at Candler School of Theology, I made a regular practice of attending the Chapel Services every Tuesday and Thursday. It was during a Thursday chapel when Dr. Richard Ward stepped to the center of the floor and "told" the text of the day in a way that brought it to life. It was the Gospel, told with integrity and accuracy but without the biblical text in hand. On that morning I experienced the Word alive as I had never experienced it before. From that day forward, I "hung onto his coattails" and reached a point where this professor became mentor and friend.

It was through the Network of Biblical Storytellers that the craft of orality became imbedded in my spirit. I know I must have been (and continue to be) the proverbial thorn-in-the-flesh for Dr. Thomas Boomershine, founder of the Network. I have called, e-mailed, and visited with Tom as I have traveled the road of personal discovery with the Story of God. To experience a biblical text so deeply it becomes "your" story goes beyond explanation. It is that connection which continues to drive me ever forward in the telling of the text and the preaching/proclaiming of God's Word.

These experiences fuel my passion for the Word and to make that Word a living Word - living among us, dwelling within us. A Word, so alive and empowering that a church was born two thousand years ago. A Word that continues to change the lives of a contemporary community which is distanced from the point of origin by years of history and technology. As Dr. William Mallard, past Professor of Church History at Candler School of Theology, would say, "the hermeneutical meeting place" is where the life of the Christian community and the line of the Gospel Story intersect. The question has to be asked: How does the gathered community of faith, the church, perceive and receive the ancient Gospel message in what Dr. Thomas Boomershine defines as a *Digital Culture*?

Cultures are labeled by their medium. Those in the caves drew charcoal etchings of hunting. The wanderers told stories around campfires. Egyptians used hieroglyphics to artistically capture life and history. The march goes on through books, photographs, sound recordings, films, television, and stereophonic and surround-sound theaters. Media is rarely discarded, simply enhanced. Today we live in a multimedia/multisensory world. We watch high-definition television. Our children are entertained by images appearing on the small screen of the computer or digital television. We communicate with digital cell phones and fast-as-lightning Internet providers. In a class on communication, I asked how many students subscribe to a newspaper or magazine, and, to my surprise, not a single student raised his or her hand. Some say we have gone back into a pre-literate environment where everything we read, hear, and watch is produced in a digital format.

The church has not escaped that change. The church has gone digital with the rapidly expanding "contemporary" worship style. This new emergent approach to worship fueled the desire to create this work from two arenas. First, the church is multisensory, and second, with the explosion of the "community church," which claims no denominational or theological anchor, many who have been called to proclaim the Word of God have little or no formal homiletical training, knowledge of church history, or liturgical understanding.

The purpose of this document is to explore the dynamics of the preaching/proclamation moment while couched in a multisensory event. This current phenomenon of "contemporary" style worship, and its impact on the established church, must be noted. However, I am not attempting to examine the entire worship experience of music, ambiance, and context. The focus is on that event which has been central to our faith since the days of the synagogue: the reading of God's word and expounding upon it in an attempt to enlighten and empower a community called to be Christ in a Post-Christian world.

In this document I will offer a methodology to create a bridge from the original text/story written in an ancient culture to the current generation using the sounds and images of the Digital Culture, which now gathers for worship in the twenty-first century. These stories are then shared in a gathered Christian community which bases its worship on an ancient text whose imagery and context are foreign to those in a Digital Culture.

I have termed this methodology Gospeltelling. The word sprang into my vocabulary while defending my Doctor of Ministry document at United Theological Seminary. The team, which included Dr. Leonard I. Sweet and Dr. Thomas Boomershine, queried my stance on biblical storytelling. When pushed to broaden the textual story, I took a hard line declaring that the text must be presented with integrity and authenticity: "I do not want to be a storyteller. I want to be a Gospelteller!" The critical difference between the two is that storytelling is entertaining while gospeltelling leads to the life-changing challenge of the Gospel message. Over time I have lived with the term, wrestling with its application. Gospeltelling embraces my conviction of authentically dealing with the biblical text and the application of an exegetical process which brings the text forward so it too applies to the proclamation of the Bible in the context worship attended by those in a Digital Culture.

This document sets the stage for methodology applying to the Gospeltelling process, a triunal event established by the action and interaction of the proclaimer/preacher, the listener/congregation, and God and God's holy text. I use the concept of Walter Ong's *senorium* to create the arena in which the proclamation moment occurs. I have selected this metaphor because the experience takes place in the context of a worship event which is, and has been throughout history, multisensory.

It has been my observation that many local churches have as their pastors persons who have a "call" to preaching/ministry and who are trying their best to be the best, using what they have acquired by osmosis from other preachers/leaders or what they have learned by self-study. Also let me say that many do not get adequate homiletical skills through seminary. (When I attended seminary, the curriculum required only one class in basic preaching.)

Tom Boomershine notes that some of the sections within this document may seem "old hat" or "familiar territory" for those who have spent years in study, but this document may be a fresh look at some new ground. I have spent my entire ministry teaching, preaching, and writing for the "common" person, most often avoiding the use of heavy theological language which may isolate those of the common vernacular. I have created this work as a short course in the history of church, worship, and preaching and in the methodology for creating a sermon/proclamation for a multisensory community.   The text has three major sections: historical background, methodological approaches, and praxis.

If there is a single thread through this document it is the thread wound around worship and proclamation. From the very beginning of the church, worship and proclamation have been cast in the hues of its own contemporary setting. Gospeltelling is another way of adapting that experience to this current generation – a Digital Culture.

Chapter 1
Sensorium:
Experiencing the Presence of God in Worship

Awe and reverence describe my impression of the small Greek Orthodox Church near the Alabama gulf coast. The arched blue ceiling is painted with gold stars – some with five points and some with six. The rose marble columns, the stained glass windows, the vivid colors of the murals and paintings go far beyond the ordinary and into the realm of the celestial. The atmosphere, saturated with the presence of the Divine, is the reason it is called a sanctuary. Here I did not need a priest or preacher to lend direction to my spiritual needs. I did not need a choir or cantor to lift my soul towards heaven. All I needed was to be in this place. To bathe myself in its silence and beauty. To experience the presence of God.

The auditorium was simple, unadorned, and dated. The tile floor streaked with shoe marks and stained with dropped snacks, desperately needed buffing. The only evidence that shifted its utility from being just an auditorium to a place of worship was a single cross on the back wall of the stage. What would one expect? It was at a campground. On this evening the room was filled with people gathered to share in community. The people sang songs of praise, and joy, and commitment. At the appointed time the congregants stood and the lights were turned off. In the darkness the voices continued to sing as five hundred small, lighted candles were lifted towards heaven. Deep in my soul I said, "God is here!" I experienced the presence of God.

Those times in life arise when one needs to escape the world in which one lives to retreat to a place where a person can attempt to put everything on hold for just a little while, a time when his or her physical, mental, and spiritual battery can be recharged. I have such a place only a few hours away. In the quiet of the forest, I listen to the cleansing, bubbling water and the conversations of the birds. I hear the rustle of leaves in the wind and smell the incense of moss and humus which fills the air. In this setting I am reminded of a song by Chris Rice which says,

Sweetest days of childhood, playing in the deep woods,
Stomping through the creek and feeling oh-so-much alive.
We're camping in the forest, we join the cricket chorus,
Hum our songs of gratitude around a crackling fire.
Out here in the stillness, I found my house of worship
With column trees and canopy of stars, here in my cathedral.[1]

Something about the Smoky Mountains lifts my spirit to another level – a level where I experience the presence of God.

In this chapter I will explore worship via a fourfold approach. First, I will define the specialness of the worship experience within the Christian community. Second, I will make a brief march through history observing the changing dynamics of worship throughout the centuries. Next, I will examine the five human senses and how these senses relate to the worship experience. Finally, I will address the attributes of the contemporary worship setting.

Where Does One Begin?

The greatest gift given to this world by those called Hebrew or Israelite or Jew is the notion that the Great Divine is not confined to a particular territory or boundary but that Yahwah God is indeed capable of being everywhere and anywhere – all the time. Even though they gathered at the Tabernacle and Temple as a "house/dwelling place" for Yahweh, they called to remembrance meeting God face-to-face in the garden, under the stars, and out in the wilderness. They lived in contention with cultures which embraced polytheism and fell from God's good grace when they turned a blind eye, but throughout the many struggles their constant cry was the Shema, "Hear O Israel: The Lord our God is one."[2]

Throughout history we have created and recreated those special meeting places. The early fathers and mothers gathered around piles of stones (etiological check-points) as they told their children stories of how humanity fell from grace, why people speak different languages, and how one was called from far away to this place. The wandering wilderness masses stood in the desert dust as they worshiped, surrounded by drapes of animal hides, their nostrils filled with the fragrance of burning flesh. In Jerusalem they processed into the splendor of massive columns, regal adornments, blazing altars, and vested priests. At each stop along the historical highway, they joined as families and communities to experience the presence of God.

In the splendor of liturgy, the community forgot the heart of God's call – to take care of each other and be faithful to Yahweh. The sacred place was destroyed. The people were scattered, and fear struck at the hearts of those who thought the story of God's people had reached its last chapter. After the exile, the people returned to rebuild the Temple and wrote down stories once held only in the memories of the faithful ones. They established places in each community to gather and talk about their relationship to God and to each other. That place, called *Beit Knesset* (House of Assembly) or *Beit Tefila* (House of Prayer), is better known as the synagogue. It was a place where communities could gather and experience the presence of God.

In the struggle for "correctness," the community shifted from seeking that "presence" to a strict, regulated obedience to the Law, filtered through the lense of the "righteous ones." Jesus had to remind them that God is not confined to the sacred space nor bound by the chains of the law. In John's Gospel, Jesus carries on a conversation with a Samaritan woman. In that dialogue the issue of where to worship is raised:

> *The woman said to him, "Sir, I see that you are a prophet. Our ancestors worshiped on this mountain, but you say that the place where people must worship is in Jerusalem." Jesus said to her, "Woman, believe me, the hour is coming when you will worship the Father neither on this mountain nor in Jerusalem. You worship what you do not know; we worship what we know, for salvation is from the Jews. But the hour is coming, and is now here, when the true worshipers will worship the Father in spirit and truth, for the Father seeks such as these to worship him. God is spirit, and those who worship him must worship in spirit and truth."*[3]

Not in the temple (Jerusalem or Samaria), or even the synagogue, Jesus declares, but wherever one seeks the presence of God, there God can be found.

After the resurrection, the new community of Jewish believers, often called "the Way," modified their worship, which now extended beyond the temple or synagogue to the homes of the "believers."

Even those outside the faith took note of their faithfulness. Pliny the Younger, governor in the Roman province of Bithynia (modern day Turkey), observed the following:

> They (Christians) were in the habit of meeting on a certain fixed day before it was light, when they sang an anthem to Christ as God and bound themselves by a solemn oath (sacramentum) not to commit any wicked deed, but to abstain from all fraud, theft and adultery, never to break their word or deny a trust when called upon to honour it; after which it was their custom to separate, and then meet again to partake of food, but food of an ordinary and innocent kind.[4]

What was the perpetuating momentum for these gatherings? As a gathered community, they found themselves in the presence of God.

When the community had outgrown the living room, they gathered in larger places with more tables and more chairs and more structure but still gathered to experience the presence of God. In the darkness of the catacombs, in fear and hiding, they broke the bread, told the stories, and experienced the presence of God. When Christianity was again able to see the light of day, they began building places to worship, which drew them back into the grandeur of the temple. Polished vessels, regal vestments, ornate appointments were once again found in the place where people gathered to hear the story, meet at the table, and experience the presence of God.

As we fast forward through church history, the meeting place went through numerous changes. We experience the shift from the dark, castle-like cathedrals to the small village chapels. We move from a time when icons and stained glass told the silent story of Jesus to a time when the wisdom-keepers began casting out anything and everything they considered idolistic or iconoclastic. Simplicity became the order of the day, yet in this broad contrast, the people still gathered to experience the presence of God.

Today we have found a plurality of sacred space. The Greek and Roman Churches surround themselves with their priceless adornments, finest wines, and purest fragrances. The Episcopal, Presbyterian, and Methodist congregate in their "sanctuaries," which speak of order and tradition. The Baptist worship in "auditoriums" with their simplicity. From the concrete block Holiness Church and the steel-walled, prefabricated building of the Community Churches, what has been the catalyst for gathering the people? It is the opportunity to experience the presence of God.

It is a special feeling, an awe-inspiring atmosphere, a magnetic pull towards the holy which keeps us going back again and again to a place of worship. I have often said that if one does not find connection with the Divine somewhere in a worship service then why bother? Some find that connection in places filled with silence. Others find their connection in a spirited song or even a song of commitment or reflection. When a choir sings an anthem or the organist plays the offertory or even when a soloist pours out his or her soul, a connection can be made. Even though often said with a smile, some may actually find a connection during a sermon.

How does one define the specialness which brings us into the presence of the holy? I do not think it occurs in a vacuum but rather at a moment supported and nurtured by many stimuli. It would be hard to define in a single word the concept which embraces the wholeness of worship. For me, the word which comes closest to the experience is what Walter Ong describes as *sensorium* – "the entire sensory apparatus as an operational complex."[5]   Worship is complex. To bring a group of people who have struggled with life for six days straight – the tension at work, the stress of family life, the anxiety of home-ownership, and the non-stop scheduling which requires a twenty-five hour day – takes something special to lift them from the mire of life's routine and place them in an atmosphere receptive to holy happenings. Yet as we enter this new millennium, there are those who wish to "worship" in places void of symbols and memories. Does the elaborate/magnificent worship place shift our spiritual sensorium from experiencing the "word" to experiencing the "space"? I think that answer must be an individual response couched in that person's perception of what it is to experience God. I do believe that worship is not monosensory but multisensory. The sensorium of worship is created and experienced via multiple stimuli.

A March Through Time

Sensorium can be used to define the multisensory experience central to Christian worship from its beginning. Philip Schaff produced a marvelous work which not only traces the history of worship within the church but also reveals the patterns of worship.

Christian worship, 33-100 AD, was literally a birthing church. It was a gathering of the faithful who had come to listen to the stories of Jesus from those who had heard the words of Jesus first-hand. The order of the gathering began with the preaching of the gospel which specifically affirmed that Christ was crucified and risen. There was a reading from the Jewish scriptures with exposition and application. Then the gathering continued with a prayer, a song, and a confession of faith (thought to be Peter's confession that Jesus was the Messiah). The service/gathering concluded with the celebration of the Lord's Supper.[6]

In the next generation (100 – 325 AD), worship began with a reading from the Jewish scriptures but now including a reading from a Letter or Gospel. By this period the church had established order and polity. The sermon or proclamation had become confined to those set apart as teachers or clergy. The message of the day ended with a doxology: *To the only God invisible, the Father of truth, who sent forth unto us the Savior and Prince of immortality, through whom also He made manifest unto us the truth and heavenly life, to Him be the glory forever and ever. Amen.*[7] The prayer time for the gatherered community was carefully composed and usually long. (This reminds me of my childhood when the preacher used the Pastoral Prayer as another forum for sermonizing. As youth we would often time his prayers to see if they were longer than the sermon.) Worship concluded with the singing of a hymn. During this period worship was often celebrated in the shroud of darkness and fear.

With the victory and conversion of Constantine (312 AD), the world experienced a major change. Church historian Geoffrey Wainwright notes, "In the second and third centuries, the Church was a relatively private community, suffering from time to time the threat and the actuality of imperial persecution and looking for the end of the world. . . . With the conversion of Constantine, however, the Church 'went public.'"[8] The church once hidden was now the church exposed. The church persecuted was now the church proclaimed. The church of small community now entered the stages of becoming global. The basic order of worship remained the same, but the lines of order and organization were drawn to perpetuate a worship pattern and style. This allowed worship to move into the realm of established tradition; in other words, we do this in worship because we have always done it this way in worship. (I have often challenged the altar guild of my church to remember that Jesus did not have purple vestments at the Passover and that the candles placed on the altar table were not there originally as a symbol of the Light of Christ but to light the text so the celebrant could read.) Leonard Sweet (theologian and futurist), observes: "All of our doctrines are at best castles in the air."[9]

In the following chapter I will use the symbol of a tree to illustrate the progressive divisions of the church. Throughout the early years the "tree" of worship was a singular trunk extending upward to the Great Schism. It is at that point the tree forks east and west. By the time of Lutheranism, and what has been termed the "Radical Sects," the tree spread its branches wide. On one side of the tree are the Lutherans, the Church of England (Anglican and Episcopal), the Methodists, and the Holiness churches. On the other side are the branches of Anabaptists, the Reformed Church, Calvinists, Mennonites, Congregationalists, and Baptists. With the expanse of the tree came the struggle to define what is "right" worship. Is it filled with historic liturgy, ancient hymns, and a strict adherence to vestment and form? Is it found in the freedom of expression within a service which changes moment by moment? Or is it found in a blend of historical understanding and contemporary relevance? The answer is yes. It can be found in each of these settings, and that is what makes corporate worship a personal matter.

The Five Senses in the Sensorium

The church has always been a contemporary church. The church has changed as people change and their perceptions change. As the church began its development and spread its wings it did so within the bounds of the current culture. The attributes of change are seen in the sensorium of the church throughout history. That sensorium is based on the sensual foundations of five human senses – sight, smell, sound, touch and taste. Worship is not a single sense event. It is multisensory. The sensorium of worship embraces all five senses.

Worship began in the darkness of back rooms and caves. In those places are etched symbols and forms which, as ancient cave dwellers, labeled the place as one not only occupied but occupied by persons of faith and conviction. The symbol of the fish (IXTHYS - ichtùs), the earliest of Christian symbols, was often carved into the stone. The Chi Ro, the first two letters of the Greek name of Jesus, was often placed on the tombs of the early Christians.

When Constantine legitimized Christianity, one of the first visible steps into the light was the community asking permission to build their churches on a Byzantine model (circa 313 AD). This type of architecture provided a large expanse of open space with thick walls, small windows, and heavy wooden roofs. The churches adorned their worship spaces with large paintings on the walls.

Over the years church architecture seemed to be on the forefront of design and function. In the Romanesque period (800-1200 AD) the architects experimented with different materials, which led to the shift from roofs of wood to stone roofs and larger windows.[10] Gothic architecture was introduced in the twelfth century, which again lifted the structures higher and provided space for even larger windows.

Standing at this place in history and glancing back, we see the broadness of style of the church as structure. As we look at the churches in our local communities, we see that some look like castles while others are literally falling down around their foundations. There are those with tall steeples pointing people heavenward while others have beautiful domes declaring that one cannot point to a God who is everywhere. Some are simple, concrete block buildings with translucent windows, and some, like Robert Scheuller's Crystal

Cathedral in California, are completely glass. Especially in the Southern Bible Belt, saturated with hundreds of denominations and theologies, we need only to take a drive to see the varied architecture where people gather.

This external, visual sense was also changing on the inside. The Byzantine style first provided large walls with pictures of Jesus and stories from the Bible. By the tenth century, the artisans took full advantage of the new-found space and filled the void with stained glass windows. These windows offered to a congregation, primarily composed of illiterate people, a visual Gospel reminding them of the biblical story. The early proclaimers often used the windows as a replacement for the written text. As they preached, they would often point to a window or scene to help the people make the connection. The windows were well entrenched in the French and German churches and later spread as the church expanded.

Many churches today use windows as a visual stimuli. Some provide beautiful biblical pictures while others simply offer the rainbow of colors which shower the worship space. When I am in the Smoky Mountains, I often worship at the First United Methodist Church in Gatlinburg, Tennessee. Since the church was built on the highest point in the town proper, a great debate arose within the congregation as to the appropriate style of window to be placed in the church. After many suggestions, one person said that they could not create a window which could adequately portray the beauty of God. So, they placed clear glass in the windows. When people come to worship, they look through the clear window onto God's own natural tapestry.

With the beauty of the architecture and window, the church also enhanced the sight sensorium by using regal tapestries, icons, and altars. Symbols were brought from the catacombs and etched in precious metals and adorned in jewels. The "old rugged cross" became an ornate symbol. The simple table where persons gathered for the sacrament found itself vested in vivid colors and set not with stoneware vessels but with jeweled appointments.

There are those who attack the artwork displayed in the worship space as being beyond the necessary. Mother Angelica, founder of the Catholic televison network the Eternal Word Television Network (EWTN), decided to build a simple place where a person could find solace. As she shared her vision, there were those who wanted to help her financially – in a big way! The simple vision eventually became the Shrine of the Most Blessed Sacrament in Hanceville, Alabama. After visiting the Shrine, which Mother Angelica calls a temple, I told someone that I finally have a visual concept of Solomon's Temple. The ornateness is breathtaking. The altar, clad in pure gold, rises above the floor and is crested with precious jewels. When often asked about the elaborate space, Mother Angelica is quick to respond that the final concept was driven by those who donated the money. That fact is so evident in the world today. Whether it is the massive tabernacle or the crude, block building, the structure we worship in is often driven by finance. And that is also, so often, the reflection of the economic status of those who worship in that church.

In the struggle of the church to create an understanding for what was "right" worship, the Calvinistic iconoclasm was shattering force of in the seventeenth century. Stained glass windows were destroyed and anything thought to be "idolistic" removed. But the church recovered, and as Christianity became more widespread and diverse, we experienced the building of grand cathedrals and humble chapels. There were ornate sanctuaries and plain meeting houses, but in each place those who gathered experienced the presence of God, enhanced by their conception of how a holy place should look.

As the church progressed in its ornateness of structure and appointment, those who led worship also became adorned. The early church leaders did not dress in robes and vestments but rather in the clothes of the common people. Probably due to the persecution and the secret nature of the early church, believers could not roam the streets in clothes which called attention to their Christianness. After the legitimation of the church and the creating of public worship spaces, the clerical dress changed. I often remind my parishioners that the example of having a special dress code for those leading worship began with God's establishment of the vestments for the priests. When God delivered the plans for a worship space, God also gave instruction on the priestly vestments, saying these special clothes "shall be a perpetual ordinance for him (Aaron) and for his descendants after him."[11]   The ancient priest was vested so the people could connect this person with the event of worship and God's commands. The common alb began to be draped with beautiful chasubles. Eventually there came an entire vestment system, which mirrored the hierarchy of church leadership. In 2005 we witnessed a marvelous display of vestment at the masses held for

Pope John Paul II. The colors and styles are indeed breathtaking.

As the church changed, so did the perception of clerical vestment. While the liturgical churches proudly displayed their vivid colors, other branches of the church tree did not hold to the same standard. There were those who wanted to go back to the early church standard, and their pastors wore "street clothes." The America Methodist tradition, birthed from the Anglican tradition, lost its liturgical element for years, due primarily to the "circuit rider" focus. A horseriding minister did not have the luxury of carrying vestments. But as the church became more established, many of the Methodist churches reached back to recover the historical liturgical element. (I usually wear a black robe and a stole which reflects the liturgical color, but in my radical nature, I also wear a cassock and chasuble on special occasion. In my opinion, vested clergy signal the holiness of the moment, but there are times when I have bowed to the wishes of a congregation and conducted worship in casual slacks and a cotton shirt.)

Again, as we worship today, there are differing views on vestment. While one pastor/priest is decked out in complete vestment, others lead worship in a cotton shirt and jeans. Again, there are no scriptural standards. Jesus did not leave us a liturgical calendar. Christ did not provide for us an order of worship. How we dress for worship is not mandated by God but is simply an avenue by which we, as proclaimers of the Word, feel a closeness to God.

The visual sensorium was enhanced by the creating of a liturgical cycle. The church year would rotate in a perpetual cycle of season and story. With the cyclical nature of worship, the vestments and paraments changed to visually signal a shift in focus. We see the regal purple colors in the Advent and Lenten season. White signals the season of Easter and holy days, while green is the color of the "ordinary" season and bold red symbolizes the Holy Spirit. The changing color cycle provides an understanding of the church year through a visual sensorium.

The eye is the window of the soul, and sight is important to worship. What we see brings us into a place of comfort or fear. Sight prepares us for what is coming and reminds us of what is past. The early church used icons and symbols as a way of aiding sight to participate in worship. Whether it is the most magnificent stained glass window or the motion of a projected image, what we see feeds our soul.

Smell accompanies sight as a sensory part of the worship sensorium. From the ancient of days incense has been burned in worship. Symbolizing our prayers rising to God as the smoke rises heavenward, the fragrance is what empowers the moment. Smell has been labeled the strongest of our senses and has been used to enhance our worship experience. Vandana Mathrani, in her article titled "The Power of Smell," writes,

> The sense of smell is the most neglected of all of the senses in humans. This is surprising, considering that seventy to seventy-five percent of what we perceive as taste actually comes from our sense of smell. More specifically, it is the odor molecules that enter the passage between the nose and mouth that gives us most of our taste sensation. Whether we smell attractive odors, such as those from certain flowers, or foul-smelling odors, such as those from rotting garbage, we do have specific behavioral responses to the smells. We can either, breathe deeply and smile, or cover our noses and look disgusted, respectively.[12]

John N. Suggit, in the <u>Oxford Companion to the Bible</u>, addresses the use of incense in the church. He notes that there were no references to the use of incense for the first four centuries of church history. Incense appears in the fifth century to represent the prayers of the people rising up to God as the smoke of the incense rises. Eventually, use of incense became part of the worship liturgy, and the liturgist would censer the people, the gospel book, the altar, and the eucharistic elements.[13]

The sense of smell has the ability to bring pleasure or pain. It has the power, with the single whiff of a fragrance, to send us to another place – a place we remember. When I enter a building where the odor of eucalyptus fills the air, I immediately think of a funeral. In the section where I will address the sensorium for the Prodigal Son, I suggest, even though it would be terribly offensive, that the fragrance of pig might drive home the despair of the son. It may be that if that odor is used to illustrate the parable, then every time people experience that aroma, they would remember the story.

A smell may take us back to our childhood joys. It may send shock waves of terror through our soul. Smell is a presence with us. We smell the incense or the fresh flowers on the chancel. We smell the eucharistic wine or the coffee brewing. Smell can be a vital part of the worship sensorium.

Sound, hearing, is part of the five senses associated with the worship sensorium. Worship is filled with sound. The chatter of people as they gather. The call to worship by the power of the pipe organ or the strumming of a guitar. The comforting words from the one called pastor/father/mother. We join with the collective voices to sing praise. There is even power in the sound of silence. The pleasure of sound is individual. It is often said that beauty is in the eye of the beholder. What one person hears, which takes him or her to the gates of heaven, may be only noise to another. Again, in God's great design of diversity, there is a sound which brings us all into the presence of God. We all do not have to hear with the same ears or approve of the same sound.

Elaine Schneider tracked the process of music in the church: "Early music was shaped by Greek, Syrian, and Hebrew influences."[14]   The singing of the Psalms were a part of every gathering. As the Christian community expanded, so did their tastes for music. The early church sang songs acappella. The form shifted in the 700's to the drone of the chant. In the Middle Ages, worship music found itself defined by where it fit into the liturgical order. "The Proper Mass was seasonal and the music depended upon the particular feast that was to be celebrated," writes Schneider. "Its movements included the Introit, Collect, Epistle, Gradual, Alleluia, Evangelium, Offertory, Secret, Preface, Cannon, Communion, and Post-Communion."[15]   Needless to say, music found its way to the core of worship.

Polyphonic choral singing arrived and was used to present the liturgical text. It is said that these pieces were often quite long and difficult for the congregation to understand. Eventually full-voiced anthems and congregational singing were added to the worship sensorium.

The inclusion of musical instruments began to make a significant impact in the Middle Ages. The Westfield Center notes the history of the pipe organ:

The organ began making its way into churches around 900 CE. Exactly how and why remains an enigma, but it appears that the organ was first used for ceremonial purposes. By the 1400s, the use of organs was well established in monastic churches and cathedrals throughout Europe. Large and small organs were in use on festival occasions and in alternation with church choirs for liturgical purposes. While most Americans may link the organ to the church, the instrument was around for more than 1100 years before it made its way into a church setting.[16]

The instrument has indeed made a major impact within the walls of the church. A significant breakthrough came in the 1930's when the Hammond company created an electronic organ which would fit into the smaller church. The "big" cathedral sound could be duplicated in the rural chapel.

With the complexity of music restricting its usefulness in worship, the Council of Trent addressed the dilemma on the proper use of music. Schneider explains, "It was decided that music for worship must be within reasonable bounds as far as its difficulty so that members of the congregation could participate."[17]

In the 1600's and 1700's some of the world's greatest composers brought their music into the church. Bach composed music for the Mass in every key. His *B-minor Mass* was the most famous. Scarlatti introduced the cantata, which used soloist and ensembles. Handel inserted the oratorio (a sacred opera) in tandem with a narrator. Handel's *The Messiah* continues to be sung in churches today. Mozart composed eighteen masses and Hayden fourteen masses.

I am always amazed at the response of people when we reach the place of discussing the music of the church. The early church sang Psalms. The mother church lifted chants from the carrels of stone cathedrals. Issac Watts brought a climatic shift to church music in the 1700's by ushering in the era of the hymn. He was so disappointed with the music in the church and complained so often that his father told him one day to stop complaining unless he could do better. And, oh, he did better! *Joy to the World*; *O God, Our Help in Ages Past*; and *Alas! and Did My Savior Bleed* are some of his most familiar hymns.

John and Charles Wesley created contemporary worship music by putting religious words to colloquial tunes. I am surprised when local congregations consider the song *Pass It On* to be a new song when it was written in the 1960's. Contemporary music is music that speaks to our spirit/soul at any given moment. There are times when

I am moved by a rousing praise chorus. There are other times when I am transported heavenward by the sounds of violins and woodwinds. Let us not forget that even Handel's *Hallelujah Chorus* was once a piece of contemporary music.

Now we use a variety of instruments, some relatively new due to current technology. The organ and piano have been replaced in many churches by the electronic keyboard, which can be programed to sound like almost any instrument or even a full-voiced choir. The church does not need a trained organist, just someone familiar with the mechanics of playing a piano to produce beautiful music. This is significant in a culture where organists are few and far between. Guitars have become standard instruments in many worship services as well as percussion and wind instruments.

Music changes with the way a community relates to each other and to God. There is a humorous story about an old country farmer who went into the "big city" and while there attended a church with a contemporary worship service. His wife asked him about the difference in how they worshiped. "Well," he said, "they sing things differently." "How so?" she asked. Trying to create a point of reference for his wife, he replied, "At our church we would sing 'The brown cow eats green grass. Amen.' But in this contemporary service they would sing, 'The cow, the cow, the brown, brown cow. Eats grass, grass, grass. The brown, brown cow eats grass. Amen.'" I sense the tension between the styles of music as extending from what the music is designed to do. The "hymn" found printed on the bound pages of our hymnal usually tells a complete story in four or five verses. The contemporary "praise chorus" appears to be more of a declaration of faith, repeated for emphasis. By way of an example, we can look at the familiar hymn *In the Garden* (also known as *I Come to the Garden Alone*) written by C. Austin Miles in 1913:

> I come to the garden alone
> While the dew is still on the roses
> And the voice I hear falling on my ear
> The Son of God discloses
>
> He speaks, and the sound of His voice
> Is so sweet the birds hush their singing
> And the melody that He gave to me
> Within my heart is ringing

I'd stay in the garden with Him
Though the night around me be falling
But He bids me go; through the voice of woe
His voice to me is calling

And He walks with me, and He talks with me
And He tells me I am His own
And the joy we share as we tarry there
None other has ever known.[18]

In contrast, we can look at the popular contemporary, song written by Rick Founds, *Lord, I Lift Your Name on High:*

Lord, I lift your name on high;
Lord, I love to sing your praises.
I'm so glad you're in my life;

I'm so glad you came to save us.
You came from heaven to earth to show the way,
from the earth to the cross my debt to pay;
from the cross to the grave; from the grave to the sky;
Lord, I lift your name on high.[19]

In the differing styles, the hymn is sung in progression – verse one, verse two, and so on. The issue here is that the leader often takes liberty to leave verses out to shorten the song. There is a humorous saying about the skipping of hymn verses: "The loneliest thing in the world is the third verse in a Baptist hymnal." In contrast, the praise song is brief and most often repeated several times. Where the power of the hymn comes from understanding the story, the power of the praise chorus comes from its drive to embed the affirmation in the soul of the singer.

Along side the liturgy and the music, drama became a way of presenting the gospel in the Middle Ages. Some say the rise of Christian drama came into being as a result of such poor preaching. The Passion Play and the Christmas Story were primary events. Miracle Plays, which came from the miracle stories in the Bible, came into being in the twelfth century. In the fifteenth century, the Morality Play became popular as an attempt to awaken humanity to the judgmental side of the faith.

Today we continue to use drama as part of our worship

sensorium. Almost every church does a Christmas pageant. I remember as a child doing small skits in Vacation Bible School to illustrate the story of the day. The church in the digital age has rediscovered the use of drama as a part of the worship service. Short skits and dramas reflect the theme or text of the day. The resources for plays, skits, and short dramas are numerous. Various companies write dramas for the liturgical year and/or topics or themes. Again, the art is used to convey the message of the gospel story and how that story applies to our lives today.

The sense of sound involves many facets of worship. The sounding of the hour using chimes or bells. The word lifted up by the liturgist. The music projected by voice and instrument. The baptism event reinforced by the sound of the water. The cry of the proclaimer declares, "Hear the word of the Lord!" So many sounds in a worship service, all calling us to focus on the Divine.

Touch includes the giving of the handshake or hug, the holding of the eucharistic elements, or even the passing of the offering plate. The New Testament church found touch a powerful sensory tool in the laying on of hands. They laid hands on each other as they welcomed persons into the community or commissioned them for specialized service. Many churches today have a special time of "passing the peace" when persons hug or shake hands as a sign of fellowship.

Touch is a bridging sensorium in that the sense describes to our consciousness the essence of what we touch. Is it hot? Is it rough? Is it pleasing? How does this feel to me? We also reverse the effect as we touch others to show our support, our sympathy, and our concern. When I offer the eucharistic elements to parishioners, I always touch their hands.

How often have we heard the words that Jesus has no hands but our hands? When we touch in the environment of worship, we become the hands and arms of Christ reaching out to others.

Taste is a sensory part of worship. The church began its ministry around the table, and that tradition has continued to this very day. There is a joke among the Methodists that when a person goes to heaven he or she has to take a covered dish to enter the gates. Sitting at the table and sharing a meal is an intimate event. In the ancient times, to share a meal was to share the soul. From that point forward a special bond was created between those at the table.

Taste is also a part of the worship sensorium as we partake of the eucharist. I often challenge my congregation when communion is served by intinction (where the participant tears off a piece of bread and then dips it into the cup); the invitation does not include a prescription for a person to take the smallest portion of the element he or she can pinch off the loaf. "We do not gather to get a little bit of Jesus," I have said. The power of the eucharist comes in the attribute of taste. Whether it is the finest bread or those cardboard tasting wafers, the sensation is there. No matter if it is Welch's grape juice or the finest wine, taste becomes a part of the worship sensorium.

The early church knew the power of taste since they gathered to eat food for physical nourishment and the elements for spiritual nourishment. There came a time in church history when food was banned from the premises – primarily to keep from soiling the carpet and staining the vestments, but now we have seen a return to the table. Many of the contemporary worship services are set around the table. In the contemporary setting, people gather, get a snack or cup of coffee, and eat and drink throughout the service. Leonard Sweet asks, "Why is it that the church always offers us the worst coffee?" So many times churches, in their effort to be frugal, will buy the store brand of coffee or day-old cinnamon rolls. Visiting a Greek Orthodox church, I was impressed when the priest pointed to the fact that they use the "best" wine they can find and the "best" bread that can be baked because nothing is too good for God. If this is indeed true, then every church should serve Starbucks coffee and "fresh today" Hostess Twinkies when they gather for fellowship.

These five senses create for us all a more powerful worship experience. The impact of sight, smell, sound, touch, and taste are used together for the greater good. As we have seen, the church, at every stage of its development, has been and continues to be multisensory.

The Sensorium of the Church of Today

In the shifting, retracing, and restating of some of the dymamics of church development, the fractured nature of what precedes this statement is a foundation for what is to come in a more intentional fashion. We need to understand the differing attributes of the church which have been faithful through the years and those which have emerged, culture by culture, to address the spiritual needs of the contemporary community.

Today we stand as a Christian community surrounded by both diversity and skepticism. We have bought into the thought that the way "we" worship is the "right" way to worship. Tensions are growing between those who struggle to find the "right" way even within denominational families. Speaking from my tradition, the United Methodist Church, we are in a battle, one side fighting to hold to the tradition which makes us Methodist and the other side challenging us to be open and explore what Christianity means to the current generation. In Leonard Sweet's book <u>The Church in Emerging Culture</u>, he notes,

> This is the ongoing struggle articulated by Frank Burch Brown: 'As a religion develops, it must orient itself both in relation to the culture of its origin and in relation to the contemporary cultures it encounters - each of which represents alternative possibilities that a religion may reject, modify, or eventually adopt.'[20]

The issue is with the concept of worship itself. Are we to remain anchored in the ancient formulas on which the church was established, or do we have the right to create our own formulas? Or, as Sweet asks, "When does Christianity become so morphed that it's no longer Christianity?"[21] We have exchanged stained glass windows for PowerPoint presentations. We have replaced stoic silence with constant movement and the acceptance of noise. We have moved away from the printed bulletin to "Spirit led," free-style worship. We have replaced our cherished hymns with bouncing choruses.

I tried to paint the picture of a sensatory experience in the image of the Malbis Church - a church which relies heavily on sight, smell, taste, touch, and sound. Further north stands a place of worship which more resembles an office complex. The Willow Creek Community Church, South Barrington, Illinois, is void of traditional symbolism. When asked about the absence of traditional church symbols (i.e. crosses, bibles, icons), founder/pastor Bill Hybels told Peter Jennings in a documentary that there is no single symbol to define Christianity, so they decided to use no symbols.[22] The place is designed more like a theater – a high-tech theater. Hybels invites people into a "neutral setting," where the spirit of God is experienced via music, drama, and effect. This style of worshiping, within the third-millennium sensorium, requires a person to focus on a central, singular point. Often the house lights are dimmed and spotlights "focus" on the moment. That focus may be the actors in a short play or a screen where words and images are projected or the preacher/presenter.

The Malbis Church meets every first and third Saturday, borrowing a priest from a neighboring church. Willow Creek attracts over 17,000 worshipers to its multiple services each week.[23]   Some churches would rather disappear through death and attrition than give up their tradition. Some churches would cease to exist if they were forced to use what they consider outdated, non-connectional, and ancient church tradition.

Successful churches cross the cultural gamut. Many churches offer multiple worship services, each having a different style. Other churches have worked to blend the traditional and contemporary elements. So what keeps people coming together for worship? It is not so much the music, or the image, or the even preaching; it is the sense of connectedness to the Divine. Somewhere in the service, whether it be in the repetition of a prayer, the effervescence of a song, or the artistry of the orator, people return to where they feel the divine connection. According to Ong, "It is tempting to reduce religion to a particular condition of the sensorium. Man is religious when the sensorium has a certain type of organization, and when it changes he is no longer so."[24]

At the risk of appearing to be heading down a road of singular style and tradition, I affirm that I am a firm believer in diversity. If anything should speak to us of the creativity of God, it should be the diversity of humankind. If we were all created with the same likes and dislikes, then there would be no need for diversity in worship, but that is not the case. When persons complain about the tension among the many Christian denominations, I simply say that I think it only shows the genius of God. When it comes to biblical theology, there is much more gray than pure black and white. Our worship styles develop out of the gray areas and in doing so open up worship to persons of every sensorium preference. Do people like to sit in silence? Do they like to jump and shout? Do people like repetition or no repetition? Do they enjoy ancient hymns or contemporary choruses? Do worshipers like their minister to be decked out in full vestment or in a cotton shirt and jeans? God's wisdom has created a place where each person can find an attachment and through the sensorium of that gathering experience the presence of God.

The danger is not in changing the style of worship to meet the needs of the gathered community but in not having that worship anchored in the soil in which this great tree of tradition is rooted. Sweet addresses the issue of tradition by using an old Latin phrase to put things in a clearer perspective: *"tempora mutantur et nos, mutamur in illis* – times change and we change with them."[25] Brian D. McLaren, pastor of a contemporary church, addresses this issue when he says,

> The oldest things (things we almost threw away, not fully apprizing their value) often turn out to be the most precious, the most worth preserving. And without preserving the whole message-method systems in our heritage, invaluable resources will be lost forever. Many of these historic spiritual ways of faith and life could be compared to rain forests. For centuries we have cut them down and replaced them with monocultural farms and pastures, housing developments, slums, or whatever, and now we discover - almost too late - that they play an essential part in our planetary survival.[26]

A primary concern is "why" we worship the way we worship. The war-cry of traditional churches against the contemporary church is that it is producing a service of consumerism. It is all about who can have the largest screens, the most powerful graphics, and the loudest music. I have to admit that there is a sense of competitiveness, but we have had that spirit of competitiveness since the birth of our own denominational families. Does it not seem odd that we name our highest, holiest, and most prestigious churches "First" church! We have tried to be better than the other church by having the highest forms of liturgy, the most pristine places of worship, the largest choir, and the grandest pipe organ. Are not those elements multisensory? The struggle is not about whether the church is heavy liturgy or light contemporary. The struggle should be whether we, however we worship, hold to the fact that Jesus should stand in the center of any worship experience. Dan Kimball, in his book <u>Emerging Worship</u>, brings all these issues to a central focal point: "A church may use multisensory worship and expensive video projectors to connect to the culture and communicate about Jesus and Kingdom living. If it ends there, however, it becomes sin. It becomes narcissistic."[27]

At a place in history labeled "pre-Christian" (since we have returned to a position where once again we are a minority being persecuted for our beliefs), we must acknowledge and affirm our diversity. John Wesley acknowledged the diversity even in his day. The Methodist church was born from diversity and created with the intention to allow for diversity always and everywhere. The Book of Discipline, which contains the doctrinal standards for the United Methodist Church, states: "It is not necessary that rites and ceremonies should in all places be the same, or exactly alike; for they have been always different, and may be changed according to the diversity of countries, times, and men's manners."[28]   In God's great wisdom we have all been created with unique characteristics. Some like coffee and others prefer soda. Some like small sports cars while others desire large sports utility vehicles. Some people enjoy the sound of a pipe organ while others get a thrill from the shrill of an electric guitar.

Today we can go to any Christian bookstore and find shelf after shelf of books designed to tell us how to worship. They tell us what colors of lights to use. They suggest the backgrounds of the PowerPoint presentations and the songs to be sung. However, for the purpose of this work, the actual worship event is not the main focus. This is but a stepping stone across the waters of worship leading toward the focus of the Gospel proclamation moment.   I will, however, offer attributes to worship settings based on the story of the Prodigal Son, which I will explore and proclaim in a later section.

It all comes to a point where we, personally, have to answer the question: Why do we worship the way we worship? We worship because we like the music. We worship because we like the fellowship. We worship because we like the atmosphere. We worship because we like the message. Simply put, we worship the way we want to worship because of the sensorium - the entire worship experience which brings us into the presence of God.

Chapter 1 Endnotes

1. Rice, Chris. 2003. *Run the Earth, Watch the Sky*, Rocketown Records, Franklin, Tennessee.
2. Deuteronomy 6:4, NRSV.
3. John 4:19-24, NRSV.
4. Pliny . Letters x 96, AD 112, *The First Christians*, http://www.request.org.uk/main/history/ romans/romans01/htm.
5. Ong, Presence of the Word,
6. Schaff, Philip, *History of the Christian Church,* http://www.graciouscall.org/books/history/ 1_ch09.shtml.
7. Scaff, http://www.graciouscall.org/books/history/ 2_ch05.shtml.
8. Jones, Wainwright, Yarnold, editors, The Study of the Liturgy, 35.
9. Sweet, The Church in Emerging Culture, 37.
10. Aaron Eichorst, *Stained Glass Design*, http://curry.edschool.virginia.edu/go/edis771/ webquest2000/student/taaroneichorst/history.html.
11. The priestly vestments are described in Exodus 28.
12. Vandana Mathrani, *The Power of Smell*, http://serendip.brynmawr.edu/bb/neuro/neuro00/web2/Mathrani.html.
13. Suggit, *Incense*, The Oxford Companion to the Bible, 301-302.
14. Elaine Schneider, *The History of Church Music in Worship*, http://www.ak.esscortment.com/ churchmusich_rksc.htm .
15. Schneider.
16. The Westfield Center Notes, *Curious Fact from the Organs History*, http://www.westfield.org/curious.htm.
17. Schneider, *The History of Church Music in Worship*.
18. Kenneth Osbeck, 101 Hymn Stories, http://www.bethquick.com/sermon7-18-04.htm.
19. Rick Founds, *Lord, I Lift Your Name on High*, Maranatha Praise, Inc, 1989.
20. Sweet, The Church in Emerging Culture, 14.
21. Sweet, 22.
22. Peter Jennings, *In The Name Of God*, ABC News,1994.
23. Outreach Magazine, Volume 3, Issue 3, May/June 2004, 55.
24. Ong, Presence of the Word, 10.

25. Sweet, <u>The Church in Emerging Culture</u>, 14.
26. Sweet, <u>The Church in Emerging Culture</u>, 194.
27. Kimball, <u>Emerging Worship</u>, 227.
28. Article XXII – Of the Rites and Ceremonies of Churches, <u>The Book of Discipline of the United Methodist Church</u>, 103.

CHAPTER 2
THE CHANGING PRAXIS OF PROCLAMATION

The worship sensorium is composed of many elements. The visual appearance of the worship space is the first sensual reception and creates the base on which all other elements rest. But even that is a relative sensorium since we all have a personal perception of what is holy, pleasing, and appropriate. Is it a place of visual beauty with vivid colors, meaningful images, and reverent atmosphere or a place of ultimate simplicity with all symbols and inferences removed? Does the music stir the soul – whatever the musical genre may be? What are the elements of celebration? Are they the finest wine and bread or the simplest grape juice and wafer? What about the time of proclamation? The time when one, called to be the voice of God among the people, shares from his or her heart and soul the message of Good News. In this chapter I will use a tree to illustrate the growth and expansion of the church. The construction of the tree will be the changing praxis of preaching as it branches into theological differences, worship nuances, and differing proclamation styles and forms.

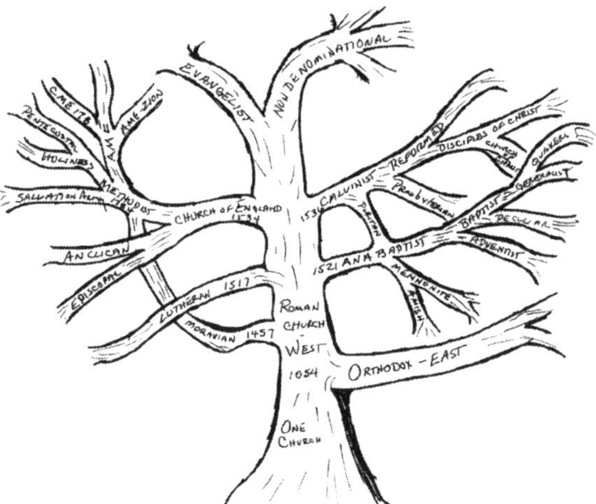

Throughout history, God's people have been exposed to a changing praxis of proclamation. Adam and Eve talked one-on-one to God as they strolled in the Garden. Apparently, they enjoyed conversation with God in the evening as they walked through the pristine greenhouse planted by the Creator. The face-to-face conversation ended in a moment of disobedience. Noah and Abraham heard the voice but apparently saw no presence as they were called to do the extraordinary tasks of saving the world and being the cornerstone of an exemplar nation. Moses experienced God in the theophany event at a burning bush and in the smoke and fire on a mountain. At this point in the history of humanity, Moses was allowed to see only the back of God, which had not been seen by human eyes since the Garden walks. The scriptures tell us that Moses had a special relationship with God, never to be equaled. In the closing moments of the Book of Deuteronomy, we read: *"Never since has there arisen a prophet in Israel like Moses, whom the LORD knew face to face."*[1]

After Moses' close encounters with God, God's proclamation to humanity took on a completely human voice. The prophets rose from the dust to shout the terrifying words, "Thus says the LORD!" They proclaimed the word of God from the desert places and from the heart of the city. They challenged communities and kings. They warned of destruction and offered hope to those in a faraway land. Even after the Temple was constructed and they danced, offered sacrifices, and paid homage to God, the proclaiming of the "word of God" was not offered only in the confines of the Temple but also outside its walls. We do not find a list of great Temple orators in the Hebrew Scriptures.

In 587 BC, Nebuchadnezer and his Babylonian forces razed the Temple and dispersed the Israelite people. When the people were allowed to return to their homeland (537 BC), worship and the study of the faith moved from a single location, the Temple, to a synagogue system embracing many local locations. (Although this is a much accepted time period for the establishing of the synagogues, there are those who move the date from the sixth century to the third century in line with the Hellenization of Israel as the word synagogue itself has a Greek root.) The synagogues brought about a major shift in the understanding of worship. It moved away from the concept of worship defined via sacrifices to a new order including prayer, study, and exhortation. O.C. Edwards notes, "The Sabbath morning service was dominated by readings from the Torah and the Prophets (the latter called the *haftarah*), a homily, weekly hymns, and the fixed prayers."[2]   The homily would be introduced by the words, "Let our rabbi teach us." Edwards has reconstructed the elements of the synagogue homily as follows:

1. The sermon begins with a statement of the first verse of the passage or several words from the first verse. . . .
2. A key word or words are explained and emphasized throughout the sermon.
3. Other words and phrases from the whole passage (not just the initial verse) are explained and repeated in the sermon.
4. Other biblical verses are cited for purposes of illustration or for developing side points, etc.
5. Illustrations are drawn from Scripture or contemporary life.
6. If scriptural illustrations are used, the biblical story is frequently retold with imaginative additions to the text.
7. In the conclusion a word or words from the opening verse are repeated to indicate the sermon is ended.
8. Frequently, the main thrust of the sermon is summarized in the conclusion.[3]

This pattern would have been in practice when Jesus returned to his hometown and took part in synagogue worship. I would imagine the service of the day was nothing out of the ordinary with the exception that they wanted to include Jesus – a hometown boy who has returned home. One account of the story is found in Luke's Gospel:

> When he came to Nazareth, where he had been brought up, he went to the synagogue on the sabbath day, as was his custom. He stood up to read, and the scroll of the prophet Isaiah was given to him. He unrolled the scroll and found the place where it was written: "The Spirit of the Lord is upon me, because he has anointed me to bring good news to the poor. He has sent me to proclaim release to the captives and recovery of sight to the blind, to let the oppressed go free, to proclaim the year of the Lord's favor." And he rolled up the scroll, gave it back to the attendant, and sat down. The eyes of all in the synagogue were fixed on him. Then he began to say to them, "Today this scripture has been fulfilled in your hearing."[4]

In this text we recognize the reading of the scripture and the homily that followed. I do not think we have the entire homily of the day. There seems to be a gap in the story for they were filled with wonder at his knowledge of the scriptures. We were not privy to that part of the service. Maybe he put the resident rabbi to shame with the depth of his understanding. I am not sure, but he said enough to make those people really angry!

Jesus taught as a traditional rabbi, using parables, wise sayings, and one-liners. We would love to embrace the concept that the Sermon on the Mount was a single sermon event giving us the experience of an extended proclamation, but it seems to be widely accepted that, in fact, it is a collection of scattered sayings bundled together. So, for the purpose of keeping the focus on the praxis of preaching, we find the first Christian sermon occurring on the day the Spirit filled the upper room. When accused of being drunk on new wine, Peter stands up and offers an extemporaneous apologetic on behalf of those drunk in the Spirit and says, "Men of Judea, and all who live in Jerusalem, let this be known to you, and listen to what I say. Indeed, these are not drunk, as you suppose, for it is only nine o'clock in the morning."[5]   From that point Peter references the prophet Joel, reminds the Israelites how Jesus was arrested and crucified, recalls the words of David, speaks of the resurrection, and ends with a challenge declaring Jesus as Lord and Messiah.

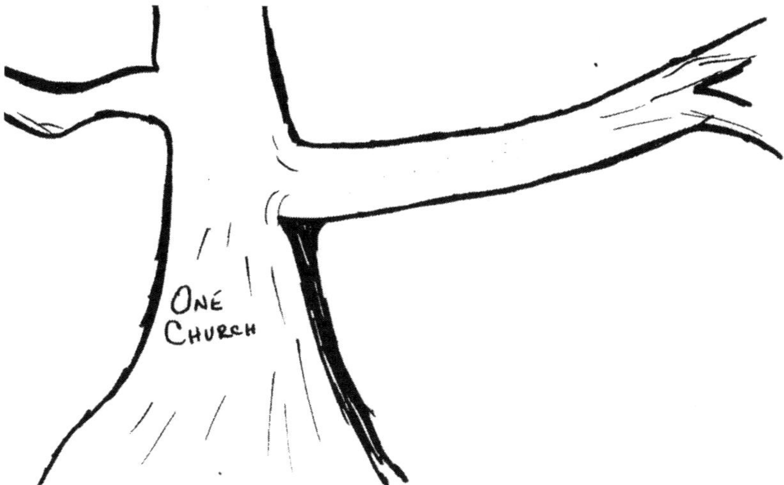

Beginning with the explosive Pentecost event, the followers of the Way went out to proclaim Jesus as Messiah. From the temple gates to the capital steps, the new community dared to offer proclamation to anyone who would pause to listen. The core of their message was the recognition of Jesus of Nazareth as the Messiah, and this was supported by references to Jewish holy writings. The first "sermons" then were thematic in nature, "Jesus is Messiah," and used the rhetorical tool of proof-texting from the ancient writings to prove their point.

The apostle Paul, an educated Roman citizen, continued the proclamation through the repeated apologetic form of evangelical pronouncement. While in Athens, Paul confronted those who were worshiping idols. He debated with those who gathered in the Jewish synagogue. He also challenged the Epicurean and Stoic philosophers. Paul eventually went to the Areopagus, or Mars Hill, where the council or court of justice met in the open air, and began his "stump preaching" saying:

Athenians, I see how extremely religious you are in every way. For as I went through the city and looked carefully at the objects of your worship, I found among them an altar with the inscription, 'To an unknown god.' What therefore you worship as unknown, this I proclaim to you. The God who made the world and everything in it, he who is Lord of heaven and earth, does not live in shrines made by human hands, nor is he served by human hands, as though he needed anything, since he himself gives to all mortals life and breath and all things. From one ancestor he made all nations to inhabit the whole earth, and he allotted the times of their existence and the boundaries of the places where they would live, so that they would search for God and perhaps grope for him and find him-though indeed he is not far from each one of us. For 'In him we live and move and have our being'; as even some of your own poets have said, 'For we too are his offspring.' Since we are God's offspring, we ought not to think that the deity is like gold, or silver, or stone, an image formed by the art and imagination of mortals. While God has overlooked the times of human ignorance, now he commands all people everywhere to repent, because he has fixed a day on which he will have the world judged in righteousness by a man whom he has appointed, and of this he has given assurance to all by raising him from the dead.[6]

We see a pattern forming, being birthed from the classical rhetorical teachings. The orator must set the agenda (the altar to the god), establish the base (God who created all things), make it relevant (that God is present – even with us), and bring it to a conclusion or, as some homiletists say, end with the "so what." The "so what" Paul proclaimed was that we are all from the God who is not unknown but known. I then picture him lifting a smile as he says, "Let me introduce you to my God."

As the faith community began to gather for assembly, the early order of worship included a time for preaching. Justin Martyr described a second century worship event as follows:

> On the day called Sunday all who live in cities or in the country gather together in one place, and the memoirs of the Apostles or the writings of the prophets are read, as long as time permits. Then when the reader has finished, the Ruler in a discourse instructs and exhorts to the imitation of these good things.[7]

Following a time of exhortation or preaching the Eucharist meal would be served. Even though we do not have the ability to hear the oral event, it has been calculated, by using the written records, that the sermon would usually last about thirty minutes.

Origen (185 – 254), often called "the first Christian systematic theologian," is also given credit for providing for us the classical form of homily. "With him (Origin) the study of Christian preaching moves from the vague to the definite," says Edwards.[8] History tells us Origen was first devoted to the study of the scriptures and did not begin "preaching" until he was in his mid-fifties. To the wonderment of scholars, apparently he preached for only three years. Speculation as to why he stopped stemmed from a feeling his sermons were not always well received. Others say his use of allegorical interpretation to approach familiar texts, his theological views on the pre-existence of souls, and his salvitic theology which allowed for the ultimate salvation of everyone could have brought about the tension which made his oratorical tenure short.

With that said, there are valuable lessons learned from the rubric of his worship. At this place in history, all worship services took place in the "church" where people had their place. The bishop and priests sat in a semicircle around the altar. Deacons sat close to the door while the congregation also sat for the sermon. Origen preached from a raised position. His sermons were usually running commentaries on a particular text. Instead of the broad stroke of the apologetic style of the apostles, he limited himself to a text and the explication of that text. Edwards writes,

> For Origen, therefore, two principles governed his interpretation. The first was the recognition that, since all Scripture is inspired by God, its meaning ought to be worthy of God and thus useful for edifying and nourishing the soul. The second principle was that nothing in the Bible—not a word, the choice of a word, even the repetition of a word— was there by accident. Everything had been placed in the text by God for a particular purpose.[9]

Some of his written sermons are forty pages long (indeed a long sermon) with the average sermon being about twenty pages in length.

A major shift occurred with the legitimization of Christianity, which was brought about via Constantine's vision, victory, and conversion. Suddenly the hidden faith of the persecuted became the visible religion embraced by the emperor. This new found respect brought about a new life within the church. Bishops were now being selected because of their wealth and political savvy. Education became a part of the process as those in leadership were schooled in rhetoric and exegesis. They became both well spoken in public and knowledgeable about the scriptures.

In the late fourth century, there arose another who brought about a shift in the proclamation event. John of Chrysostom, often labeled "the Golden Mouth," brought to his ministry the background of philosophy and rhetoric. He was preparing for a career in the Roman civil service to write or "phrase" imperial documents. He began his work in the church as an aid and was later given the task of reading the lectionary readings of the day. During this time he became very familiar with both Jewish and Christian texts (Old Testament and New Testament writings). He was elevated quickly in the hierarchy of the church to become a bishop. It could be said that he was the first to introduce the elements of contemporary tastes into his church, for it has been recorded that his congregations often broke out in applause when he preached. J.W.C. Wand wrote that the event was so intense "and the congregation's attention was so closely engaged that notices had to be put up in the church warning hearers to beware of pickpockets."[10]

Unlike Origen's allegorical style, John was quite literal in his verse-by-verse, exegetical style of preaching. He raised questions about the authorship of the Gospels and deduced that Matthew was originally written in Hebrew and that Mark wrote his gospel to be sent to Egypt. He questioned the accuracy of Matthew's genealogy and pointed out other inconsistencies within the four Gospels.

He seems to follow in the footsteps of John the Baptist, one crying out with a vengeance for people to change their ways and take care of the community. We can feel the passion in this selection from one of his homilies on accountability:

> The gold bit on your horse, the gold circlet on the wrist of your slave, the gilding on your shoes, mean that you are robbing the orphan and starving the widow. When you have passed away, each passer-by who looks upon your great mansion will say, "How many tears did it take to build that mansion; how many orphans were stripped; how many widows wronged; how many laborers deprived of their honest wages?" Even death itself will not deliver you from your accusers.[11]

The term "Golden Mouth" came from an experience that we cannot recapture. People can read all the sermons they want, but the true power of a sermon, an oral form of transmission, is found in its original hearing. We can attempt to resurrect it with our oral presentations, but we lack his passion, his empathy, his aura. Edwards describes it this way:

> His sermons were transactions with a live congregation, not words on paper, much less translations of those words into other languages. We can know nothing of his electrifying presence as he sat in his chair in the ambo, much nearer to his audience than if he had preached from the customary position of the bishop's chair behind the altar in the apse. The interaction with the congregation, mentioned by Broadus, cannot be recaptured. What John's delivery was

like, the way he used either his body or his voice, is unavailable to history. What the voice that came from the Mouth of Gold sounded like cannot be known. And those who experience his words only in translation cannot guess at the magic of sound or the precision of expression in his choice of words. All that is left is the judgment of his contemporaries that he was the best there was at a time when oratory was one of the most highly developed and critically appreciated art forms there was.[12]

Before we leave the Early Church, we must visit Augustine. His life and writings have been examined on many levels which could, and have, filled volumes. However, for our purpose, one of his major contributions was writing one of the first homiletics textbooks. *De doctrina christiana,* often translated "Concerning Christian Doctrine," has been defined by Edmund Hill as simply "Teaching Christianity." There are four books within this document: <u>Fundamentals of Christian Doctrine</u>, <u>Interpretation Required by Ignorance of the Meaning of Signs</u>, <u>Interpretation Required by the Ambiguity of Signs</u>, and <u>The Christian Orator</u>.[13] The titles themselves offer an insight to Augustine's approach to preaching and interpretation.

Where John of Chrysostom looked at the literal interpretation of Biblical text, Augustine believed it was all about signs or things. He once said, "The whole Bible, therefore, is about using everything else as a means to enjoy God, to love God. God is to be loved for the sake of God, and neighbors are also to be loved for the sake of God. The Summary of the Law – love God and love your neighbor – is the key to interpreting the whole Bible."[14] Augustine believed the Bible was a book of signs that needed to be interpreted. In the light of that interpretation Augustine issues three tasks or duties of the preacher/orator: to prove, to delight, and to move. These are also the steps in classical rhetoric as identified by Cicero, who stated that the orator must be able "to prove things to the audience, please them, and sway their emotions."[15] The final action was the most important since he felt the ultimate goal of preaching was the conversion of persons to Christianity. It must have been an effective style since on occasions as many as two thousand people gathered in the congregation to hear his message.

As children we played a game called "Simon Says" in which one child calls out directions to the others to take steps forward or backward. A player can move only if the leader says, "Simon says." If a player moves otherwise, he or she is out of the game. So, "Simon says take a giant step forward." That step reaches across the medieval period of the church. It is not that there were no important developments during that period, for there were major developments. Christians were prolific in building churches and they excelled in producing beautiful art and music. However, it was during this period that the mass, the worship event, became almost exclusively a function of the clergy. In an article titled "An Introduction to Worship," the author writes, "The sermon often was either not included at all or it consisted of a moralistic exhortation not based on the lessons. Besides the fact that the mass was in Latin, the words of the canon (the eucharistic prayers) were usually spoken so softly the congregation couldn't hear."[16] Duane Gardner says,

> Sermons, on those rare occasions when they were included in the mass, were moralistic, filled with apocryphal illustrative stories and anecdotes, and had rather little to do with exposition of the Scriptures. Because the weekly Mass was performed in Latin, which was practically a foreign language to the majority of the European people, and because there was not yet an efficient means of reproducing the text of the Bible, the world had been cut off from the written Word of God for several centuries. . . . Medieval worshippers were, in general, uncomprehending observers to the worship of the clergy with no access to Word or Sacrament.[17]

This is not to say that all preaching was either misunderstood or incomprehensible. As a part of the Carolinian reform, preaching was expected to be used for the propagation of the Christian faith through the hearing of the people. In 813, the Reform Councils also were quite insistent that not only preaching should be used to instruct but also should be done in the vernacular. There were those who excelled in the field of preaching, such as Bernard, who is said to have been "above all, a talker." Yet the standard edition of his works total 3,500 pages, of which two-thirds of that material is considered sermonic. Also in this time came the emergence of women such as Hildegard of Bingen, who enhanced her preaching with images drawn from her many visions. She embarked on four different "preaching tours," where she preached before both laity and clergy, lifting up the theme of the need for salvation.

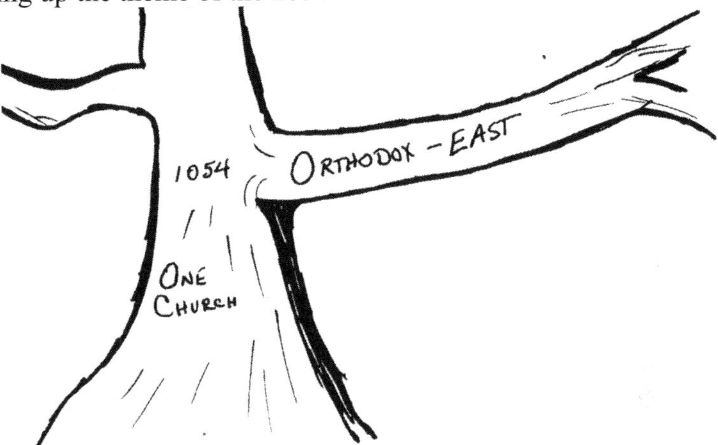

A crack in the vessel of God came in 1054 with what is titled "The Great Schism." The reasoning behind the schism varies according to which side of the story a person hears. Issues over the Petrine Doctrine (accepted by the West and rejected by the East), issues of celibacy of the priesthood, and the use of unleavened bread in the Eucharist were some of the listed reasons. Beyond these were issues of power and politics, which became the wedge that severed the Universal Church. Until this schism, the "tree" was a single trunk, but now it began to add branches, especially in a Western direction.

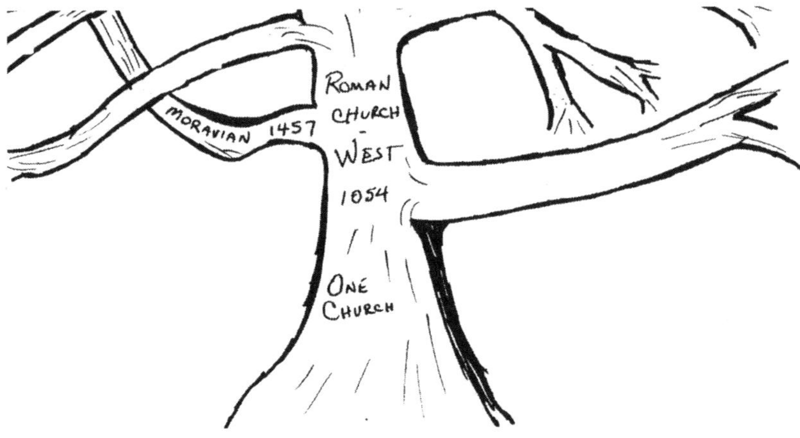

The first branching from the Western trunk is also the oldest surviving Protestant community. The *Unitas Fratrum*, or commonly called the Moravian Church, was birthed in Bohemia in 1457 AD. D. H. Tripp describes the new form of worship:

After some three weeks of preparatory services and both private and public confession, the rite opens with a hymn, a prayer, and a sermon. During a further hymn, the priest and deacons (no special vestments) approach the Table, which is already prepared. The people are exhorted to penitence, then kneel for a prayer, Our Father, and a hymn. They rise for the absolution. The Instituion Narrative is chanted to consecrate the elements. After priests and deacons have received, the people approach at the priest's invitation, . . . During the communion, hymns on the passion are sung. Thanksgivings, intercessions, and blessings complete the service.[18]

Pietistic in nature, the Moravian worship included a generous application of hymns and singing. The branch almost died under the pressure of the Roman Catholic Church, and if it had not been for a small, stalwart group, it would not have survived. A sudden rebirth came in 1727 through the ministry of Count Zinzendorf. Zinzendorf had a great love for music and a marvellous talent for preaching. The church immersed itself in song and hymn, many written for specific services or even extemporaneously to fit the occasion. His gift of preaching was described just as that, a gift. It was said that he did very little preparation for a sermon and spoke directly from his strong convictions. He said of himself, " . . . as soon as I begin to speak, . . .I feel the coals from the altar. I am sensitive to the varying moods of my hearers. They often shed tears, which is the case even with the soldiers among them."[19]

In the thirteenth and fourteenth centuries, there arose an explosion of preaching. With the expanding population and better farming techniques, which produced the need for better trade systems and prosperity, cities were expanding and the masses were now in close proximity. With these newfound congregations came the need for those to serve the people, and the friars developed a system for training preachers. The Pope himself recognized the need for the expansion of this ministry. The preaching brothers called Dominicans, after Dominic who established the order, were to provide a foundation for homiletical training. The goal of that training was to prepare persons to combat the evils of heresies. Pope Innocent III, in 1210, extended that permission to the Franciscans with the stipulation that their preaching should be concerned with penitence and not doctrine.

From these two orders came a new way of homiletical understanding on how the sermonic plot should manifest itself. The process was illustrated with a tree and its branches. Otto A. Dieter, in a fifteenth century manuscript illumination, notes that we see

> its trunk and limbs are labeled to show which parts of the tree correspond to which parts of a sermon. About halfway up, the trunk separates into three large boughs, each of which later divides into three limbs. This tree represents the way that a sermon should be based on a text, which, like the tree, is divided into three points, with each point then broken down into three subpoints.[20]

Sermons were often broken into numbered parts so that the congregants could follow the homiletical plot. This method is still used today. Several years ago I pastored a church which gathered with two other community churches of a different denominations for a time of worship and fellowship. I do not know if the pastor was trying to impress us with his knowledge, but he began his sermon with a short introduction and then started to number his points – "Point 1 … Point 2 … Point 3." I finally became weary when I heard him say, "and number 17."

As in our time-conscious age, there were cautions about preaching too long. To keep the sermons within reason, the preachers would have a friend signal them when their time was up. The Black church still uses that method as the congregation begins cheering on the pastor by saying, "Preach it!" and "Go on, brother/sister!" When the congregation feels the proclaimer has come to the end, or needs to end, they cry, "Bring it home!" All of this lends some validity to the statement I have heard from my parishioners: "You can preach as long as you want but we leave at noon."

Not all preaching came from clergy. There were those lay

persons who felt the call to proclamation. John Wyclif (also Wycliffe) was one such lay preacher. A fellow of Merton College and later a master of Balliol, Wyclif received a bachelor's degree and later a master's degree. During this period a lay person could receive income from a church appointment without actually having to provide any services for the said church. It was through this arrangement that Wyclif received the major portion of his income while at Oxford. It took him eighteen years to receive his doctorate.

Wyclif focused his work on the doctrine of the holy scripture, and, in time, he produced a complete commentary. In 1377-78, he produced a treatise titled *On The Truth of Sacred Scripture,* which argued that the Bible is inerrant and therefore should be used as a standard to measure all claims of truth. Holding to that bold statement as a foundation, he then claimed that the Bible should be available to all Christian people. With that burning fervor, Wyclif translated the Bible into English (actually two translations, as the second was a more refined edition). He also proposed the creating of a new religious order of Poor Preachers, who would preach to the people from the English version of the Bible. It could have been that Wyclif thought himself to be too scholarly to relate to common people, so he provided training for lay persons to proclaim the Gospel in dual vernacular – the Word of God and the word of the preacher. Michael Hines says, "Wyclif surrounded himself with a group of trained preachers. Once instructed in the basics, Wyclif sent these 'Lollards' or 'Poor Preachers' out to preach. These simple men asked nothing and gave much. They proved an adequate contrast to the worldly monks who begged much but gave nothing."[21]

Wyclif's religious and biblical concepts place him as a precursor of the forthcoming Reformation. Edwards states, "We expect great things of Wycliffe and his school; the study of his extant sermons has, however, disappointed those who wish to see in him a 'precursor' of the Reformation. Though his Latin sermons are wholly scholastic in character, the English sermons are a practical, popular proclamation based upon the Bible." [22]   His preaching legacy was carried out by those whom he sent out as persons who "prepared the ground for the reformation in England, by establishing groups of men who were accustomed to radical ideas on the church and authority within it, and who regarded the text of the Bible in the vernacular with special reverence."[23]

Another shift in proclamation came with the works of Desiderius

Erasmus, who wrote *Ecclesiaticus* (circa 1535), which became the best seller of the decade. John W. O'Malley calls the work "the great watershed in the history of sacred rhetoric."[24] Erasmas called his sermon style *concio*. It was not the rhetoric of the educated and sophisticated but rather developed for the common or ordinary persons and their understanding. His task was to train persons to preach on the vernacular level. Erasmas said, "If elephants can be trained to dance, lions to play, and leopards to hunt, surely preachers can be taught to preach."[25] But it is more than just words:

> The preacher should exhibit purity of heart, chastity of body, sanctity of deportment, erudition, wisdom, and above all eloquence worthy of the divine mysteries. Let him remember that the cross will never be lacking to those who sincerely preach the gospel. There are always Herods, Ananiases, Caiaphases, Scribes and Pharisees. There are men of Ephesus who incite the mob and there are those like the Jews before Pilate who cried, "Crucify him! Crucify him!"[26]

Even though it is said that Erasmus never preached himself, his call to move the heart of the sermon from the lofty heights to a common level continued to move the Gospel back to its rightful place – among the people.

A contemporary of Erasmas, Martin Luther, posts the third branch on the Church tree. In 1515, Luther had his "tower experience," which provided the springboard for his conflict with Rome. He described his experience as follows:

> I greatly longed to understand Paul's Epistle to the Romans and nothing stood in the way but that one expression, "the justice of God," because I took it to mean that justice whereby God is just and deals justly in punishing the unjust. My situation was that, although an impeccable monk, I stood before God as a sinner troubled in conscience, and I had no confidence that my merit would assuage him. Therefore I did not love a just and angry God, but rather hated and murmured against him. Yet I clung to the dear Paul and had a great yearning to know what he meant. Night and day I pondered until I saw the connection between

> the justice of God and the statement that "the just shall live by his faith." Then I grasped that the justice of God is that righteousness by which through grace and sheer mercy God justifies us through faith. Thereupon I felt myself to be reborn and to have gone through open doors into paradise. The whole of Scripture took on a new meaning, and whereas before the "justice of God" had filled me with hate, now it became to me inexpressibly sweet in greater love. This passage of Paul became to me a gate to heaven.[27]

From this event comes the awakening to justification by faith. He declared that Christians do not earn their salvation but salvation is freely given by God. Salvation by works was based on the premise that people "earn" salvation and could even lessen the days in purgatory if they worked hard enough or paid enough in indulgences. I will not go further into the church history arena but rather point out the contribution to preaching Luther offered.

Luther placed the office of preaching above the office of sacrament. He also put that priority to praxis. For Luther, preaching the Word of God was bringing about John's concept of the "Word" among us:

> Therefore, any preacher who finished a sermon should not pray for the forgiveness of its deficiencies, but should say, 'In this sermon I have been an apostle and a prophet of Jesus Christ.' Anyone who cannot boast like that should give up preaching, 'for it is God's Word and not (the preacher's) and God ought not and cannot forgive it, but only confirm, praise, and crown it.'[28]

He often preached as many as four times a day and felt that it was through preaching that faith was communicated. Luther said, "This is the gist of your preaching: Behold your God!
Promote God alone, his mercy, and grace. Preach Me alone."[29]
Luther believed in the oral process and preached from an outline. His style, basically expository, was not verse-by-verse but rather meaning-by-meaning, what he termed the *Sinnmitte* (center of meaning), *Herzpunkt* (heart point), or *Kern* (kernel). His sermons were more an effort to extract the meaning of the text rather than to explain the text through a critical, theological, exegetical process.

Edwards writes,

> In the preaching of Luther, then, there was a perfect marriage of content and method. His grammarian's analysis of the text allowed him to discover its meaning for the congregation, and the form of the *contio* enabled him to direct that insight powerfully to their attention. And the doctrine of justification itself was not just something to be explained; it was a call for a response, a demand for a decision. [30]

At almost the same time in Switzerland, Ulrich Zwingly began to develop his theology independent of Luther but in the same general direction. He issued a theological battle cry, *sola scriptura* – scripture alone.

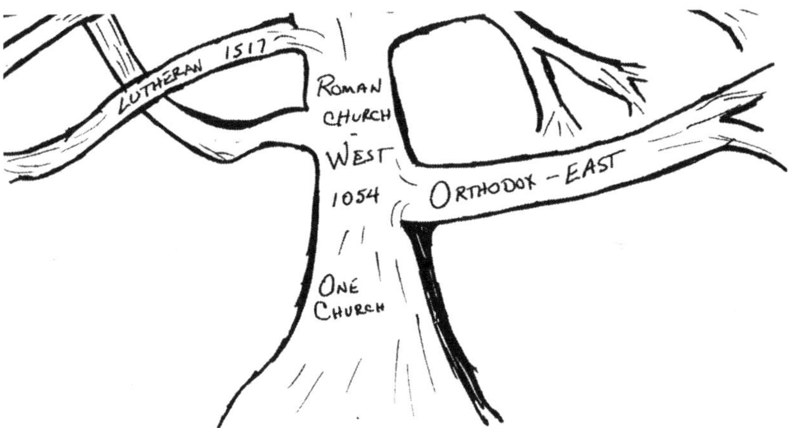

Suddenly we experience a blossoming of the Church tree. This tree which remained a single trunk for over one thousand years suddenly began sprouting branches in rapid succession. First, the Great Schism between the East and West was followed by the Untitas Fratrum (the Moravian Church) circa 1457 and the Lutheran episode, circa 1517. The historical timeline moves upward and outward as the Church Tree spreads its branches in diversity and global influence. From this point I will follow branches rather than a chronological pattern. I must also place a disclaimer here since there are many variations on the exact nature of the "branching" and even disputes within individual denominational histories concerning which family belongs to a which branch. The illustrations inserted are, to the best of my understanding, a reasonable representation of church history.

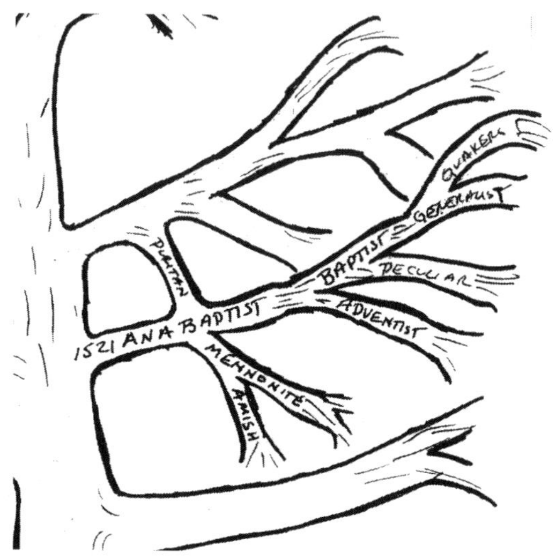

With the Reformation moving "full steam ahead," there arose a holy boldness in religious defiance. The Anabaptist, "the rebaptizers," revolted against a state sanctioned church. These persons insisted that the church one attends and is baptized in should be completely separated from civil government. They were also egalitarian that promoted the equality of women with men and the inclusion of all social groups – the rich, the educated, the poor, and the illiterate.

They renounced infant baptism, affirmed free-will of the believer, and used the Bible as the standard by which one was to measure and evaluate every situation in life.

Melchior Hoffman, a leather-dresser, became a prominent preaching figure in the early Anabaptist movement. One who had stepped from branch to branch, first a Lutheran, then a Zwinglian, and finally an Anabaptist, he began a "dooms-day" proclamation announcing that the "Day of the Lord" is near and seemed all-consumed with his apocalyptic sermons. He proclaimed a self-fulfilling prophesy about his imprisonment. I have been unsuccessful in locating one of Hoffman's sermons, but in the historical documents explored, he must have been an explosive orator.

Under the influence of Hoffman's preaching there rose another who would create further branching in the Church Tree. A Dutch Catholic priest by the name of Menno Simons began struggling with the doctrines of the Roman Church, especially the issues of papal infallibility and transubstantiation – where the elements actually became the "real" body of Christ. To abbreviate the historical issues, in time Menno Simons became the leader of a group later called the Mennonites. His preaching was described as evangelical rather than sacramental and seemed to be less aggressive than his mentor Hoffman.

A schism took place in the Mennonite congregation led by Jakob Ammann, who had issues with several of the doctrines embraced by the Mennonite Church. Setting a differing standard, Ammann called for uniformity in dress which included the style of hats, garments for the body, shoes and stockings. He also taught against the trimming of the beard and attending services in the state church.[31]

The Amish worship experience and "preaching style" is captured by Brad Igou:

> Worship begins at about 8:00 a.m. and usually lasts over three hours. Hymns are sung from the AUSBUND, a special hymnal used by the Amish. (We will devote our second article in this series to the music at church services.) There are usually three to seven preachers and bishops at a service. These men retire to a room during the singing to decide who will be preaching the two sermons that day.
>
> Around 8:30 a.m., the first sermon begins. Since people may be seated in different rooms, the ministers may move about somewhat as they preach. Some ministers present their message in a sort of chanting, sing-song manner, in the Pennsylvania German dialect, with Scriptures in High German. It is not unusual for much emotion to be shown, and tears are not uncommon. The pitch and tone of the voice vary for emphasis. As in any church, different preachers have different styles. This first sermon may last about thirty minutes.
>
> Scriptures are read and they kneel for silent prayer prior to the main sermon. This sermon is longer, sometimes over

an hour. Ministers often quote a passage from Scripture and then talk about it. Sermons are not written in advance. It is quite amazing that these "untrained" clergy can deliver such powerful, emotional messages to their congregations. Leading a right life in the eyes of the Lord, resurrection, and the idea of "judge not that ye be not judged" are some common themes. Some also like to preach from the Old Testament.

After the main sermon, the other ministers usually make short statements that add to or emphasize what has been heard. There is about another half hour of prayer and singing. The Amish have a booklet outlining the hymns and Scriptures to be used at each service. Readings from the New Testament chapters of Matthew predominate, with Luke and John rounding out the year.[32]

In these early settings, where sermons seemed to be extemporaneous, we do not have texts to examine but rather we have the "spirit" in which they were presented. Here in the Amish community the style seemed to be more of a teaching event which even had the element of rebuttal and response.

Returning to the main branch, we see that the Anabaptists evolve toward the group now defined as simply Baptist (circa 1630). In the Americas, (under the general religious title of Puritanism) Roger Williams, founder of Rhode Island, basically made the province a Baptist state. Yet this group, now independent by virtue of distance, began to realign their theology.

Although most of their core beliefs were retained via their Anabaptist roots, they were also influenced by Arminianism which allowed for the element of free-will verses the elect. The debate over these theological issues brought another split in the branch. The Generalist Baptists retained their Arminian views which stated that Jesus had died for all humanity. The Particular Baptist held to a strict orthodox Calvinistic theology which declares that Jesus died only for those "elected" or predestined to be saved.

Perry Miller writes in *The New England Mind* concerning the preaching style of the era:

The Puritan sermon quotes the text and "opens" it as briefly as possible, expounding circumstances and context,

> explaining its grammatical meanings, reducing its tropes and schemata to prose, and setting forth its logical implications; the sermon then proclaims in a flat, indicative sentence the "doctrine" contained in the text or logically deduced from it, and proceeds to the first reason or proof. Reason follows reason, with no other transition than a period and a number; after the last proof is stated there follow the uses or applications, also in numbered sequence, and the sermon ends when there is nothing more to be said.[33]

The style seems more scientific than evangelical.

The Baptist branch expands into a variety of particular divisions, but with my experience, the core of the Baptist preaching continues to be a call of urgency and repentance. Their sermons are enthusiastic and often thematic. Their preaching is marked by using many verses from all over the Bible to provide evidence of their conviction (proof-texting).

In 1650, the Annabaptist branch divides again when a young cobbler's apprentice by the name of George Fox left his vocation to pursue a drawing toward the Spirit of God. At first he wandered among many of the religious communities and finally became convinced that all of the various sects in England were wrong in their theology. Fox observes,

> If God does not dwell in houses made by human hands, how dare anyone call those buildings where they gather 'churches'? They are in truth no more than houses with belfries. . . . Hymns, orders of worship, sermons, sacraments, creeds, ministers – they are all human hindrances to the freedom of the Spirit.[34]

Taking the path of the Generalist Baptist (all are open to the salvitic plan of God), Fox said each person has an inner light, no matter how dim, which allows a person to understand the call and presence of God. As his followers grew, the movement was first called "Children of Light," but Fox preferred the name "Friends." However, as with other religious branches, those outside the community gave them the name by which they are more easily recognized – Quakers.

Their worship service did not include a formal structure since they felt that structure hindered the freedom of the Spirit. Without order or form also meant without the typical sermon, but instead, anyone – men and women – would get up when they felt the presence of Christ urging them to speak.

The final branch begins in the 1820's when a Baptist minister from Vermont decided that the church had misinterpreted the correctness of the Bible and, by taking some material from Daniel, Genesis, and other Scripture, devised a method by which he predicted that Christ would return in 1843. William Miller developed a following, but when the apocalyptic date passed many left the community. The small group that remained found a common spirit in an English branch named the Seventh-Day Baptist (circa 1650). These Christians thought that the Church had left the teaching of the Bible by switching the day of worship from the seventh day to the first day of the week. Their worship service is ordered since they note that God had order and hates disorder and chaos. The <u>Seventh-Day Adventist Handbook</u> names the order as music, announcements, call to worship, prayer, offering, children's ministry, scripture reading, and public testimony.[35] The Adventists also take an ordered view of sermon/preaching and offer a pattern of eight rules required for effective preaching as follows:

1. Know Christ Personally
2. Preach Biblically
3. Preach Relevantly
4. Preach Positively
5. Prepare Early
6. Organize Logically
7. Speak clearly
8. Plan Annually[36]

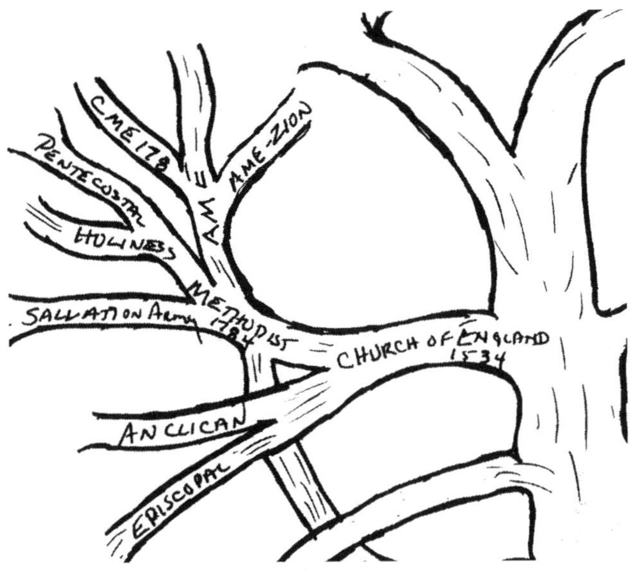

We now move up the tree to the next major branch with begins with a king who, because of a personal disagreement with the Roman Catholic Church, decided to establish his own church. Henry VIII sought out an annulment from a marriage which was not granted by Rome. After much debate and tension, in 1534 Parliament put in place a series of laws including that anyone was prohibited from making contributions to the Roman Church, that the marriage of Henry and Catherine was not a "true" marriage, and that the king was the supreme head of the Church of England. In order that these were adhered to, anyone who did not obey and accept would be held guilty of treason. When we think of Henry VIII and the Church of England, we have the idealistic concept of a smooth break and the branch simply grows in a new direction. That could not be further from the truth, and the turmoil and tragedy experienced on the road to full independence and recognition embattled the entire nation.

The Book of Common Prayer, a work produced by Thomas Cranmer (1549 AD), who became the king's chief religious advisor, established the differences between Rome and the new church. In particular, Cranmer changed the view in the Eucharist liturgy from the concept of the host literally becoming the body and blood of Christ to the understanding that the elements do not change and that communion was a celebration of the presence of Christ. Also the services were set in the vernacular, giving the English people a liturgy in their own language. Another issue was the setting aside of the issue of clerical celibacy, and the clergy were allowed to marry. (Note that in the history of the Church of England that some of these issues were tossed back and forth according to who sat on the throne. When Mary came to power she was sympathetic to Rome, and clergy were ordered to "set their wives aside.")

With the Reformation in full swing throughout Europe, a new day was dawning which embraced the common men and women and their faith.   There arose what has been termed "a plainness in preaching." The people sought for religion to be relational, realistic, and experiencial. With the advances in science and philosophy and the end of many of the wars, society was changing to be primarily driven by the mercantile class rather than the aristocrats.

A new feeling was being birthed from Oxford under the influence of the Wesley brothers, John and Charles, and George Whitefield (circa 1730's). In their "Holy Club," the members sought a closer, more experiencial experience, and their theological approach and preaching style often kept these men on the outside of the church and not in the pulpits. Whitefield had such a fervor with his sermons, which called persons to a rebirthing experience, that he had been accused of driving fifteen people mad through his preaching.

Whitefield's success was supported by his personal gift of communication. He had a voice which could be heard by large audiences and had the power to put feelings into the words. According to Edwards, "The actor David Garric is reported to have said that Whitefield could 'make his audiences weep or tremble merely by varying his pronounciation of the word Mesopotamia. . . . I would give a hundred guineas if I could only say 'O!' like Mr. Whitefield.'" [37]

Whitefield's approach to preaching appealed very much to the masses on two fronts. First, he preached without the use of notes, and, second, he usually preached outside. This style was later termed "field preaching." He created a pattern for his sermons which is still in use today. Termed "evangelical preaching," the sermon was based on a short biblical text and included a short introduction, background information on the text, the listing of the major points, and a conclusion.

The Wesleys were kindred spirits with Whitefield (all priests in the Church of England), and their Holy Club or "Bible Moths" provided for them a place to practice the discipline of prayer, self-examination, and works of mercy. The adherence to these disciplines led to the labeling of their systematic approach as "Methodist."

Wesley had had an encounter with the Moravians on a return trip from Georgia noting their faith and confidence in God during a storm. When searching for a way to acquire this solace, an Oxford colleague, Moravian Peter Bohler, challenged Wesley, "Preach faith until you have it; and then because you have it, you will preach faith." The turning point for John Wesley was his heart-warming experience at a Moravian society meeting on Aldersgate Street, May 24, 1738. Wesley joined Whitefield in his field preaching, and in his remaining fifty-two years of life and ministry he preached more than forty thousand sermons.

Wesley made a distinction between the oral preaching event and the written sermon. "Live" preaching was primarily for both the proclamation of God's word and the invitation to become a believer. "Written" sermons were chiefly constructed for reflection and nurture. Even though he did not have the public attraction of Whitefield, when he died at the age of eighty-four, there were in Great Britain about seventy thousand Methodists and also about sixty thousand in the Americas.

It was the Revolutionary War that brought about the division in this branch. Since many of the churches in the Americas were Anglican with priests loyal to the Mother Country, after the war there came a void of those ordained to word and sacrament. The Methodists in America were preachers only and could not administer the sacraments. When the bishop of London refused to ordain persons for ministry in the Colonies, Wesley took a radical approach by personally ordaining Frances Asbury and Thomas Coke for service in 1784. Even though Wesley never intended a division of the church, the inevitable occurred, and the Methodist Church was born. Birthing from the early Methodist meetings, often those called to preach did not have the advantage of formal education. James Kiefer relates the following story:

> … although Wesley found it natural to approach the Gospel with habits of thought formed by a classical education, he was quick to recognize the value of other approaches. The early Methodist meetings were often led by lay preachers

with very limited education. On one occasion, such a preacher took as his text Luke 19:21, "Lord, I feared thee, because thou art an austere man." Not knowing the word "austere," he thought that the text spoke of "an oyster man." He spoke about the work of those who retrieve oysters from the sea-bed. The diver plunges down from the surface, cut off from his natural environment, into bone-chilling water. He gropes in the dark, cutting his hands on the sharp edges of the shells. Now he has the oyster, and kicks back up to the surface, up to the warmth and light and air, clutching in his torn and bleeding hands the object of his search. So Christ descended from the glory of heaven into the squalor of earth, into sinful human society, in order to retrieve humans and bring them back up with Him to the glory of heaven, His torn and bleeding hands a sign of the value He has placed on the object of His quest. Twelve men were converted that evening. Afterwards, someone complained to Wesley about the inappropriateness of allowing preachers who were too ignorant to know the meaning of the texts they were preaching on. Wesley simply said, "Never mind, the Lord got a dozen oysters tonight."[38]

The Methodists of early years were preachers of God's Grace and were influenced by the Armenian theology that God's Grace is open to all. That being the case, there rose a philosophy that wherever there was a post office there would be a Methodist church. Circuit Riders were the roving clergy who carried out their missionary duties on horseback and proclaimed the Gospel in what Wesley termed "plain preaching." In the diversity of the Methodist church today, preaching style crosses the cultural gamut. United Methodist Churches are pastored by well-educated Elders with seminary degrees and those who are called "lay pastors" with little or no formal biblical or religious training. Therefore, even today, Methodists hear sermons that challenge the intellectual and also hear sermons which "harvest oysters."

From the beginning of Methodism, slavery was an issue of religious conscience. In 1779 Asbury sent a manifesto to the Methodist Conference asking the conference to set as a standard that no Methodist would own slaves. This motion did not pass. Again, in 1796, it was moved that Methodists would not be allowed to sell slaves at a profit, and once slaves had worked off the cost of their purchase, they were to be freed. These issues met with great resistance since a stronghold of Methodist membership was held in the South where slaves were considered a necessary part of production and economy.

In the 1780's, two black clergymen began recruiting other blacks to attend the Methodist Conference. Freeborn Garrettson and Harry Hoiser called for blacks to attend the establishing Christmas Conference of 1784.

In 1816 a freed slave by the name of Richard Allen purchased land in Philadelphia and established a Methodist Church for blacks. Allen built the Bethel Church, adopted the Methodist Book of Discipline, and created the African Methodist Episcopal Church. Later, in 1820, a separate group in New York asked that the AME send them a bishop. When the AME refused, that group started their own new branch calling themselves the African Methodist Episcopal Church – Zion. (AME – Zion)

This branch took another turn in the 1870's. Eight Methodist Episcopal Conferences in the south convened in Jackson, Tennessee, to form a new denomination for blacks. The new denomination was originally called the Colored Methodist Episcopal Church, but in 1954 the name was changed to the Christian Methodist Episcopal Church or the CME.

Black preaching is in a field all its own. It is not stuffy or high but creative, inspiring, and researched. It is evangelistic and energetic. The Black Church blended the educated-expectation of Methodism with a touch of Quaker and Amish attributes. Even though the service is structured, the worship service flows with the "moving of the Spirit." Their sermons are often antiphonal. In some traditions, the preaching moment is carried by the solo voice of a preacher. In other traditions, the sermon is lifted by an acknowledging word spoken out loud, or the "amen." However, in the Black Church, the congregation helps the preacher preach the sermon. They often tell the scripture story along with the preacher. There are times when the congregation finishes the sentences of the one leading a chorus of word and response. Tony Campolo tells of how the preacher gets his or her grading on the spot. If the preacher is doing well in the sermon, then he or she will hear the words "preach on!" lifted up from the congregation. If the preacher is struggling with the sermon and the people cannot find a place to join the preacher on the road of the Gospel, he or she may hear a call, "Lord, help him or her!" In either case, the black congregation seems more in tune with the Biblical texts and feels comfortable becoming a part of the proclamation moment.

Out of the concern for slavery and other social ills, in 1840 a group attended the Methodist Conference calling for the abolishment of slavery. When the conference failed to pass the resolution, Orange Scott, along with about twenty thousand followers, formed the Wesleyan Methodist Church and took their spirituality to a new level. Calling for a return to the spirituality of John Wesley, their theology embraced a two-step salvitic plan (Saved and Sanctified). They also declared the inerrancy and infallibility of the Bible. This church took on the attributes which labeled them a Holiness Church. Recovering some of the Pietistic thought, they sensed the call to separate from "the world" and went to the battlefront over slavery, abstinence from tobacco and alcohol, and secret societies. Their preaching was spirited and driven with a sense of urgency – save the world before Jesus comes back. They were known for their powerful revival services and camp meetings where the preachers could put even the hymnal under conviction.

Taking the holiness tradition to a deeper level, the Pentecostal Church was formed in the early 1900's. This church took all the attributes of the Holiness Church and added to it not only a more energetic style of worship and music but also claimed that if one was really saved one could prove it by the speaking in unknown tongues. The preachers were fiery and loud and often shouted the people into a religious frenzy. They were portrayed by their black suits, their white shirts with a thin black tie, and their big floppy Bibles. Often the preachers would get so enthusiastic that they would begin to gasp to get enough air to continue their boisterous proclamation. Their sermons are often thematic, and they, like some before, spend a lot of sermonic time proof-texting their material from all over the Bible.

Before I leave the Methodist branch, let me briefly address the church without a church. In 1865, a London Methodist clergyman decided to move outside the church to minister to the poor and struggling. William Booth intended to build a "church" for these people but later realized those outcasts of society did not and would not feel comfortable there. So Booth established mission stations where people could come and hear him preach. It is said that his fiery sermons and use of vivid images often stirred people to change their lives and, in turn, do their part in fighting "sin." Booth said, "While women weep, as they do now, I'll fight; while little children go hungry, as they do now, I'll fight; while men go to prison, in and out, in and out, as they do now, I'll fight; while there is a poor lost girl upon the streets, while there remains one dark soul without the light of God, I'll fight; I'll fight to the very end!"[39]　It was out of this fervent spirit that those called "Salvationists" would go into the street and fight for the lost souls. Empowered to do spiritual warfare and established in a military-like structure, the name of the organization became the Salvation Army.

In examining the branch which begins with the Church of England, one sees that there are two forks. One fork takes the path of the Anglican Church in England and the Episcopal Church in America but maintains a common bond. The other branch is that of Methodism, which creates a number of off-shoots. Now we return to the trunk and explore another major branch, the branch created by the Calvinists.

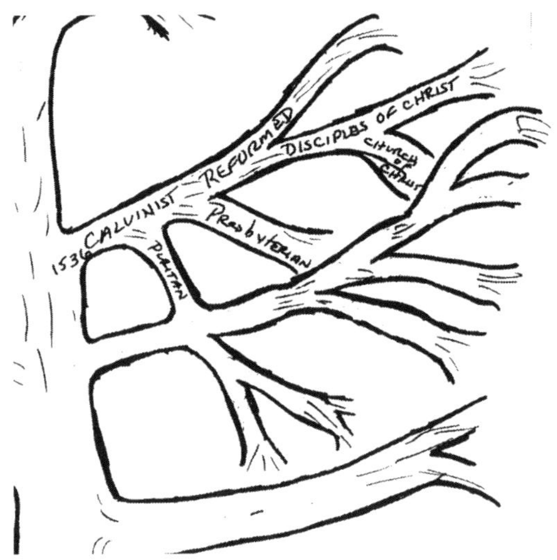

Almost at the same time the Church of England forms, change was taking place in Switzerland through the work of Urich Zwingli. In his reformation efforts, two major shifts were brought into the worship setting. The first was that the liturgy designed by Zwingli centered around the sermon and not the eucharistic event. The second shift was the move away from the lectionary readings and instead began a process of preaching through the books of the Bible. These elements formed the base from which John Calvin's theology was the springboard for the Reformed Churches. Theologically, Calvin believed in the doctrine of predestination which states that the Church is the body of the Elect. The Elect are those who are predestined by the love and free will of God to salvation, faith, and grace. As the Armenian view states, everyone has the opportunity to receive God's grace; Calvin's theology of predestination describes justification as the decision and act of God alone, and we can do nothing to change the will and intent of God.

Calvin was very vocal about the act of preaching, which he felt was the channel by which the Holy Spirit speaks to the church. He also said that when the Spirit speaks to the preachers, the Spirit reveals to them only what is already in the Scripture, and the Spirit is not the creator of new revelations. Calvin says, "Clearly not everyone is fitted to be a pastor; knowledge of the Scriptures and soundness of doctrine must be joined with faithfulness, zeal, and holiness.. As important as any of these, however, and without which no man can be a good preacher, is the gift of teaching."[40] John K. Baumann observes, "At the center of Calvin's pastoral work was the preaching of the gospel. He preached or lectured every day with two sermons on Sunday. He believed that preaching was to be a pastoral event through which souls could be brought to the full and liberating assurance of faith. For Calvin, preaching was meant to open the door of the kingdom of God to the hearer."[41]

Calvin took his own words seriously and was indeed a true Bible scholar and an excellent orator. When speaking about the use of rhetoric he said,

That eloquence, then, is neither to be condemned nor despised, which has no tendency to lead Christians to be taken up with an outward glitter of words, or intoxicate them with empty delight, or tickle their ears with its tinkling sound, or cover over the Cross of Christ with its empty show as with a veil; but, on the contrary, tends to call us back to the native simplicity of the Gospel, tends to exalt the simple preaching of the Cross by voluntarily abasing itself, and, in fine, acts the part of a herald.[42]

T.H.L. Parker outlined a typical Calvinistic sermon as follows:

1. Prayer.
2. Recapitulation of previous sermon.
3. (a) Exegesis and exposition of first member.
    (b) Application of this, and exhortation to obedience or duty.
4. (a) Exegesis and exposition of second member.
    (b) Application of this, and exhortation to obedience or duty.
5. Bidding to prayer, which contains a summary of the sermon.[43]

This pattern seems to offer a thread of continuance from one sermon to the next sermon. Also, it could create, for some, a sense of expectation.

The Reformation was also going strong in Scotland, and the leader of that reformed movement was John Knox. Catholic Mary had ascended to the throne in England and was determined to reclaim the Roman Church. Knox found himself in exile in Geneva where he spent time with John Calvin. From exile, Knox continued his part in the Protestant Reformation, and while he was not present in Scotland, his spirit was felt. It is reputed that Mary Queen of Scots said, "I fear the prayers of John Knox more than all the assembled armies of Europe." Eventually the Roman Catholic Church was displaced by a democratic church called the Presbyterian Church of Scotland (circa 1560).

Knox was known for his "aggressive" style of preaching and nick-named the "Thundering Scot." *The Reformed Theological Journal* published the following:

All his days Knox was a diligent student. In his letters he sometimes describes himself as 'sitting at his books' and as studying the gospel by the help of the Fathers 'and among the rest Chrysostom.' He had a competent knowledge of Greek and learned Hebrew during his years in Geneva. He never wrote out his sermons but obviously studied them very carefully, as is witnessed by the fact that he could reproduce their substance days and even years after they had been preached. We learn from an incidental remark in his 'Admonition to England' that his method was to speak from a few notes made on the margin of his Bible. The framework of his sermon was thought out beforehand and, from his own memoranda as well as the reports of others, he clearly had premeditated the precise words by which he would express his thoughts.[44]

The branch suddenly makes another strange twist and connects the Annabaptist and Calvinistic branches. The labels were varied: Baptist, Reformed Baptist, Reformers, or Campbellites. The movement seemed to have been started by Kentuckian Barton W. Stone when he ended his Presbyterian ties in 1804 to become a "Christian only." Thomas Campbell and son Alexander, Scotch Presbyterians, founded the Brush Run church in 1811, whose theological foundation was the "the restoration of pure primitive apostolic Christianity, in letter and spirit in principle and practice." Later these two joined forces and came to be known as the Disciples of Christ. A later blend formed the Christian Church: The Disciples of Christ.

Alexander did not think the church went far enough in its primitive ways and formed a "non-instrumental" church called the Church of Christ (circa 1810). The preaching is more of a teaching event, selecting a text and then supporting that particular text with proof-texts.

I end the branching of the tree here, but this is by no means an all-inclusive map of church history or of preaching style. Today there has risen a new church which claims no connection and most often goes under the heading of a "community church." Again, in a reformative manner, members of this new church wish to step away from the baggage of historical liturgy and rhetoric. Their style of preaching varies as do the churches in style and theology. I will address the contemporary approaches of preaching in the next chapter.

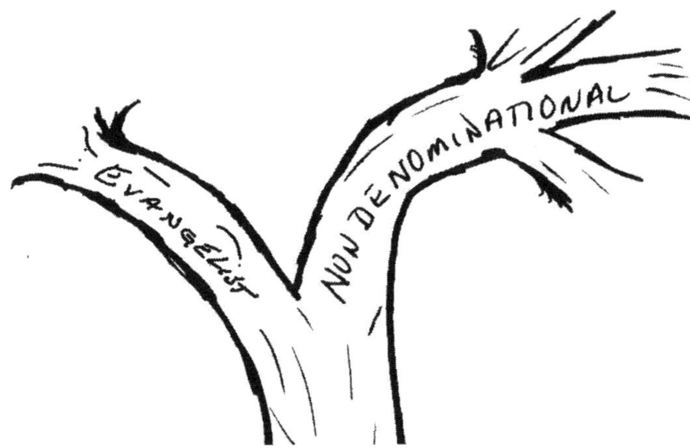

As we reach the top of the tree, there are those who, even though they have denominational connections, seem to find a place outside church labels. These "evangelists" have called the community to higher standards and have used the tool of preaching to address the masses.

Jonathan Edwards (1703-1758), as a part of that Great Awakening, is an early example of powerful, evangelistic preaching. We often think of Edwards as "larger than life" when in fact he was described as tall and gawky. However, he moved the people with his preaching. One person wrote:

> It was not due to theatrics. One observer wrote, 'He scarcely gestured or even moved, and he made no attempt by the elegance of his style or the beauty of his pictures to gratify the taste and fascinate the imagination.' Instead he convinced 'with overwhelming weight of argument and with such intenseness of feeling.'[45]

When we talk of Edwards we immediately go to his sermon "Sinners in the Hands of an Angry God." The imagery is so vivid that some say the congregation could smell the brimstone of Hell as he was preaching. An illustration from the sermon affirms the feeling:

> The use of this awful subject may be for awakening unconverted persons in this congregation. This that you have

heard is the case of every one of you that are out of Christ.- That world of misery, that lake of burning brimstone, is extended abroad under you. There is the dreadful pit of the glowing flames of the wrath of God; there is hell's wide gaping mouth open; and you have nothing to stand upon, nor any thing to take hold of, there is nothing between you and hell but the air; it is only the power and mere pleasure of God that holds you up.[47]

It was reported that he would preach this sermon holding his notes in his left hand and rarely looking up from the text, but the power of his imagery often caused persons to faint from fear.

Charles Finney (1792-1875) followed in the footsteps of Edwards, plastering on the minds of his listeners the images of hell and damnation that would be their destiny if they did not turn from their evil ways. And Billy Sunday (1862-1935) was known for his sharp-witted 69 quotes: "When I hit the devil square in the face some people go away as mad as if I had slapped them in the mouth. I'm against sin. I'll kick it as long as I've got a foot, and I'll fight it as long as I've got a fist. I'll butt it as long as I've got a head. I'll bite it as long as I've got a tooth. And when I'm old and fistless and footless and toothless, I'll gum it till I go home to Glory and it goes home to perdition!"[47]

These preachers often drew large gatherings that required meetings to be held outside local churches. In the humid South, "brush arbors" were used. Nothing more than a roof on stilts and a sawdust floor, these arbors were the site where many people would gather to hear the fiery evangelist night after night. With the popularity of evangelists like Billy Graham, sports arenas and football stadiums became places of worship.

Billy Graham modernized the evangelical event by using large community choirs, inviting well-known celebrities, and using media. He would ask for a response from those at the service to come forward to pray and then turn toward the television camera and ask those "at home" to say the "Sinner's Prayer."

Television and media have created a world-wide church for many evangelists. Jimmy Swaggart, Jim and Tammy Faye Baker, Jerry Farwell, Robert Scheuller, Kathryn Kuhlman, and Joyce Meyer are just a few who have excelled in this new church environment.

Today the media has become even more personal as many

churches produce their worship services on the Internet, making contact as easily as the click of a computer mouse. The sermon is multi-media using the preacher's words and images to enforce the topic.

I will address the contemporary styles and issues of preaching in the next chapter with one final thought before leaving this march through history. It appears that at each branching of the tree there are two constants. First, each branch is caused by a shift in theological understanding. Second, this shift is accompanied by a passion for proclaiming the Word of God. For me, the worth of the tree is known by its fruit. The fruit of this tree can be experienced by seeing all those who found a way to connect to God - in whatever form of worship and under whatever style of preaching they choose. If there is wisdom, if there is purpose, if there is intention in this branching tree it is this: God has provided a place for everyone to experience the presence of the Divine through worship and the word.

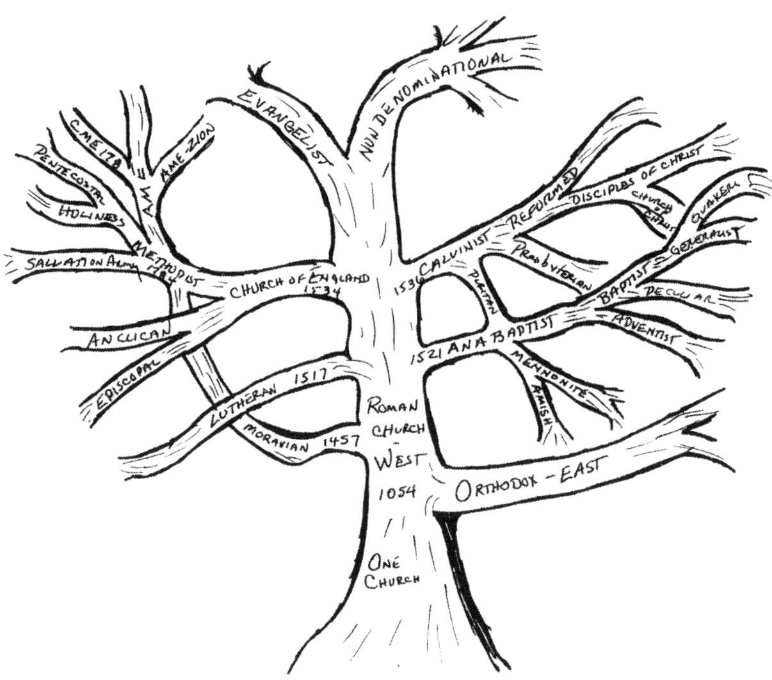

Chapter 2 Endnotes

1. Deuteronomy 34:10 NRSV.
2. Edwards, <u>History of Preaching</u>, 9.
3. Edwards, 10 – 11.
4. Luke 4:16-21 NRSV.
5. Acts 2:14-16a NRSV.
6. Acts 17:22-31 NRSV.
7. Leslie William Barnard, <u>St. Justin Martyr: The First and Second Apologies, 1 Apol</u>. 67. , ACW, no. 56.
8. Edwards, 31.
9. Edwards, 40-41.
10. Wand, <u>The Greek Doctors</u>, 68.
11. Gonzalez, <u>The Story of Christianity, Volume 1</u>, 197.
12. Edwards, 81.
13. Hill, *On Christian Doctrine*, http://ccat.sas.upenn.edu/jod/augustine/ddc1.html.
14. Edwards, 106-107.
15. *Internet Encyclopedia of Philosophy*, http://www.iep.utm.edu/c/cicero.htm# The%20Orator.
16. *An Introduction to Worship*, http://wwwfac.cord.edu/ministry/worship_sheets.htm.
17. Duane Gardner, *The Role of Preaching In The Covenant Renewal Liturgy*, 2003, http://www.hornes.org/theologia/content/duane_garner/preaching_in_the_liturgy.htm.
18. Jones, Wainwright, Yarnold, ed. <u>The Study of Liturgy</u>, 250.
19. Spangenberg, <u>The Life of Nicholas Lewis Count Zinzendorf</u>, 124.
20. Otto A.Dieter, *"Arbor picta: The Medieval Tree of Preaching," The Quarterly Journal of Speech*, 51, 1965, 273.
21. Michael Hines, *Late Medieval and Renaissance Reformers*, http://www.christianchronicler.com/history1/late_medieval.html.
22. Edwards, 254.
23. Edwards, 255.
24. John W. O'Malley, *"Erasmus and the History of Sacred Rhetoric: The Ecclesiastes of 1535,"* <u>Erasmus of Rotterdam</u>, 29.
25. Edwards, 275.
26. Bainton, *Erasmus,* 268-69.

27. Paul Halsall, *Modern History Sourcebook: Martin Luther: The Tower Experience, 1519*, http://www.fordham.edu/halsall/mod/1519luther-tower.html.
28. Edwards, 287-288.
29. Edwards, 289.
30. Edwards, 298.
31. Mennonite Historical Society of Canada, http://www.mhsc.ca/index.asp?content= http://www.mhsc.ca/encyclopedia/contents/A463ME.html.
32. Brad Igou,, *Amish Religious Traditions*, http://www.amishnews.com/amisharticles/ religioustraditions.htm.
33. Perry Miller, *The New England Mind*, http://guweb2.gonzaga.edu/faculty/campbell/ enl310/sermstru.htm.
34. Gonzales, 198-99.
35. *The Seventh-Day Adventist Handbook*, http://www.chat11.com/cgi-bin/wiki.pl?search =Seventh-Day+Adventist+Elder+Guide+To+Preaching.
36. *The Seventh-Day Adventist Handbook*
37. Edwards, 435.
38. James Keifer, http://www.satucket.com/lectionary/Wesley.htm.
39. http://www.swordofthelord.com/biographies/booth.htm.
40. Edwards, 315.
41. John K. Baumann, *John Calvin as Preacher*, http://department.monm.edu/classics/ Speel_Festschrift/baumann.htm.
42. Edwards, 315-316.
43. Edwards, 316.
44. "John Knox, Preacher of the Word," *Reformed Theological Journal*, 1987, http://www.freechurch.org/douglas/ eouglas8.htm.
45. *Christians Everyone Should Know*, http://www.christianitytoday.com/history/special/ 131christians/edwards.html.
46. Jonathan Edwards, *Sinners in the Hands of an Angry God, Application*, http://www.jonathanedwards.com/sermons/ Warnings/sinners.htm.
47. *Billy Sunday Quotes*, http://www.geneamondson.com/ mission/billysundayquotes.html.

CHAPTER 3
THE PRAXIS OF PROCLAMATION

Chapter One examined how the vision of persons shifted the sensorium of worship moving from a single room and a few fearful disciples to majestic cathedrals colored with stained glass and then forward to the twenty-first century arenas filled with electronic wonders. Chapter Two explored church growth and the power of the individual who, through an awakening or epiphany, changed the sensorium of the church in worship, word, and theology. Chapter Three shifts from the broad worship/church venue to the differing approaches to the proclamation moment, commonly called the sermon.

From the earliest gatherings of the people, the "word" has been presented in differing voices. The Buddhists have a saying: "There are as many paths to Nirvana as there are Buddhists." The same could be said about preaching/proclamation. The goal of each path is the same – offering the Word of God to be heard and experienced. There are as many styles and personal approaches as there are those lifting a voice to proclaim the "word." In this chapter I will explore some of those paths which lead to the sensorium of proclamation: Fred Craddock and the Inductive Method, Eugene Lowery and the Sermonic Plot, Charles Rice and Preaching as Story, Henry Mitchell on Black Preaching, Patricia Wilson-Kastner and the Single Image, and Thomas Troeger on Imagining the Sermon.

Fred Craddock - The Inductive Method

I remember entering the large lecture hall, which was filled with first-year seminary students, on the campus of Emory University. Almost hidden behind the large scientific table at the front of the room, Dr. Fred Craddock began his class in preaching by pointing to a student and asking, "How did you get here?" Still in shock at being singled out, the student smiled and said, "A car." "No," Dr. Craddock said and began to explain how he may have arrived there in the class. I do not remember the exact directions, but it went something like this: First, you walked out the front door of your apartment, went down the sidewalk to your car and climbed in. You cranked the car and drove to the parking deck on campus. Leaving your car, you walked down the hill and crossed the main street only to climb back up a hill to the classroom building. Entering the front doors, you went down the hall to the lecture hall. Opening the door and looking around, you chose a place to sit, and that is where you took your seat. From that beginning I realized preaching is more than just a word; it is a journey.

Craddock's process of sermon development is labeled the inductive method. This method is presented in two particular texts – As One Without Authority and Preaching. It was from Preaching Dr. Craddock first called us to an awareness of our task as proclaimers of the Gospel. Dr. Craddock says, "Faith makes one believable. ... Passion makes one persuasive. ... Authority is that which gives one the right to speak. ... and grace is that which keeps the speaker a listener."[1]   I remember so well the day he told us, "When you enter the pulpit, keep one eye on the manuscript and one ear tilted toward God."

Craddock makes the distinction between methodologies. A deductive style of preaching moves from general to particular; the inductive process is the reverse of that movement. Craddock illustrates this when he says that "in induction, thought moves from the particulars of experience that have a familiar ring in the listener's ear to a general truth or conclusion."[2]

Lock Bowman, Jr. illustrates the methods as follows:

General Truth

Particulars of Experience

Particular Applications

General Truth or Conclusion

Deduction

Induction[3]

The inductive process is two-fold. First, there is the connection between the preacher and the text. Craddock's methodology breaks this part of the proclamation process into seven subtitles. The first is the actually *selecting the text*. If the preacher/proclaimer is from a church with a liturgical background, the text each week is offered with options of Old Testament, New Testament, Psalms, and Epistle readings. If he or she is from a non-liturgical church, the selection is up to the preacher/proclaimer and the choices span sixty-six books of canonized text. Both choices have their pro's and con's, yet the fact remains: in Craddock's inductive method one must first start with a text.

The text selection is followed by *reading the text*. Craddock says, "The Scripture for the sermon is read, several times silently and at least once aloud."[4] This is followed by the third step, *establishing the text*, which means that one explores and compares the text to find different wording or translation differences. Sometimes translators selected different English words when translating a Hebrew or Greek word. At issue here is the trustworthiness of the text, whether it is reliable and accurate in its translation.

The fourth step is *determining the parameters of the text*. Craddock explains: "One should ask if the text selection is a unit having its own integrity, and therefore providing focus and restraint for the sermon. ... Observing the parameters of a text often allows the preacher to isolate and treat smaller units of material without fear of violating the meaning of the text."[5] Knowing where the text fits into the larger story gives the proclaimer a place of tension. What happens just before and just after the particular text creates the color of the text. For example, was this pericope preceded by a crisis event which set the stage for this story? To what action did this story lead? This moves to the fifth action, *setting the text,* in its several contexts. What is the historical setting? What is the literary connection with the connecting stories? What theological issues are present?

The sixth step in the text process is *becoming aware of one's point of contact with the text*. Craddock leads one to ask, "At what level did I engage with the text? ... [and] ... At what point did I identify within the text?"[6] Craddock suggests first that one seek to find the connections that may create a connection with other biblical texts and images. This is followed by the exploration of oneself and where this text will engage not only the proclaimer but also the listeners.

The final step is *putting the text in one's own words*. Being able to restate the text creates the springboard which propels the text toward the listener. Craddock suggests reducing the text to a single sentence: what the text says followed by the question "What is the text doing?" Is it a text of celebration, confirmation, or correction?

Once these steps have been taken – and taken to heart – Craddock says that a person can now determine what he or she has to say about the text. In this process of evaluation, exploration, and reflection, one should look for the *eureka* moment. In his class, Craddock also calls this the *ah ha!* Through this textual process – guided by study and prayer – something should surface which provides the catalyst leading to the enthusiastic creation of the sermon's composition.

The second section in the inductive process is connecting the text and the listener. Once the *eureka* has been experienced, how is that conveyed to the listener? Craddock offers six options. The first is the *direct and uncritical transfer* of the text. He says, " This method consists simply of reading a passage of Scripture and then treating it in the sermon as though it had been written with this audience in mind."[7]

The second style is the *allegorical interpretation* of the text, where one says, "I hear what it is saying, but what is the message behind the story?"

This is followed by the third style, the *typological interpretation:*

> Typology is a way of addressing present listeners with the ancient text by discerning in that text events of conditions having clear correspondence to those of the listeners. ... In other words, something occurs or is experienced in the history of Israel or of the early church which is a type of present community's experience, and therefore, present listeners can properly be instructed, encouraged, or warned by that past occurrence or experience.[8]

The fourth style is the interpretation of the *intent of the text.* Sometimes a text makes clear what the true message may be. For example, a parable told by Jesus seems so innocent in its presentation, but in the end the listener realizes it was told to or against a particular group of people. Dr. Vernon Robbins, Professor of Religion at Emory University, suggests many of Jesus' parables were familiar stories. When Jesus began to tell the parable, the people would think, "I have heard this one before!" Then Jesus would insert a surprise ending, or what Robbins calls a "hook." Craddock uses the parable in Luke 18:1-14 as a unique example which sets the stage for the hearing and the application before Jesus tells the story:

> *He also told this parable to some who trusted in themselves that they were righteous and regarded others with contempt: 'Two men went up to the temple to pray, one a Pharisee and the other a tax collector. The Pharisee, standing by himself, was praying thus, "God, I thank you that I am not like other people: thieves, rogues, adulterers, or even like this tax collector. I fast twice a week; I give a tenth of all my income." But the tax collector, standing far off, would not even look up to heaven, but was beating his breast and saying, "God, be merciful to me, a sinner!" I tell you, this man went down to his home justified rather than the other; for all who exalt themselves will be humbled, but all who humble themselves will be exalted.' (Luke 18:9-14)*

The author of Luke sets the parameters to whom this parable is directed – those who trust in themselves.

The fifth approach is that of *thematic interpretation of the text*. What issue or concept is found within a chosen text? Does this particular text address issues about money or greed or faith? This leads to the sixth and final interpretation, *translation of the text*. Craddock instructs, "This method seeks to interpret by freeing the text to speak to the reader or listener by removing barriers that are due to difficulties in language. . . . the task is to release the text upon the listener's ear by translating it into the language of the listener."[9]

From this point the preacher/proclaimer begins to actually construct the message. Craddock explains: "The effectiveness of the sermon soon to be preached will in large measure depend on two factors: (1) the preacher's capacity to anticipate that listener's response, and (2) the preacher's capacity to shape the sermon to meet the challenge of that response."[10] Craddock's methodology moves the person developing the sermon to create a single statement or theme sentence which summarizes what he or she wants to say – usually birthed from the *eureka* moment. Once that is accomplished, the entire sermon from introduction to the last word should point toward that single statement. He does not embrace a single style of delivery but encourages speakers to use a variety of presentation styles. The sermon moves from a specific experience to an experience wide enough to embrace all who hear. Then Craddock reminds us of this: "The preacher enters the pulpit undergirded by several fundamental convictions about the experience of that moment. First and foremost is the belief that this message will make a difference."[11]

What is not evident in the construct of the sermon is what makes sermons come alive in the moment. For example, Fred Craddock with his marvelous sense of humor draws people into his trust. At a conference at Camp Sumatanga in the hills of north Alabama, Craddock commented on the beauty of the facility: "This place is so beautiful! I went out for a run this morning. I do not run every morning, just when I get the urge. I am up to six miles. That is the cumulative total for the past five years." To share laughter is to give permission to others to engage in emotion of the moment.

Craddock also has the wonderful ability to paint creative images to bridge the ancient text to the contemporary ear. In describing a less than appropriate sermon, Craddock said it "went over like a concrete cloud." In one of his most powerful sermons, he addresses our mortality and illustrates "death" as "one who slips on his bloody boots and walks down the center stripe of the highway."

Even though the inductive method seems so structured, Craddock's use of allegory and metaphor brings to life and into life the lessons of the Gospel. He insists we be aware of the creative detail – the paying-attention-to-the-process which is a part of my methodology of Gospeltelling.

Craddock's Inductive Method

Preacher and the Text	**Listener and the Text**
» Selecting the Text » Reading of the Text » Establishing of the Text » Parameters of the Text » Setting of the Text » One's Point of Contact with the Text » Putting the Text in One's Own Words	» Direct and Uncritical Transfer of the Text » Allegorical Interpretation of the Text » Typological Interpretation of the Text » Intent of the Text » Thematic Interpretation of the Text » Translation of the Text

Eugene Lowery - The Sermonic Plot

As Craddock's inductive method is more attune to the process leading to the proclamation moment, Eugene Lowery moves us toward a style of delivery. Dr. Lowery served as Professor of Preaching for over thirty years at Saint Paul School of Theology in Kansas City, Missouri. Though I have not attended one of his homiletics classes, I have experienced his presence at the piano keyboard as he lectured on the topic of "Jazz Theology."

Lowery's approach to narrative preaching moves away from the standard "three points and a poem" format to more spatial process. He shifts the paradigm from time to space and replaces the idealistic content with story. Lowery says this process of development is "an *event-in-time*, a narrative art form more akin to a play or novel in shape than a book."[12] His thesis is that a sermon is not a "thing" but rather an "ordered form" which moves in time. It is not shifting points but a journey.

Lowery says there are four aspects to a narrative style of preaching/proclamation. The first basis is *setting*. Where does the story take place? Where do we imagine the location of the story? There are times when the location is fixed and specific; there are times when the story setting is implied and requires our imagination. We may move to that place by saying, "In a land far, far away." In the setting the creator establishes a specific place and time for a sense of concreteness. We paint for the listeners the location so they can visualize where they are – in the desert or the jungle or the city.

The second aspect is *character*. Who are the characters and what are their relationships with each other? As Craddock asked the question about how the student arrived at class, Lowery says we must ask questions which give life to the character. It is not simply a person – but a person with relationships.

Action is the third aspect of the narrative style. Story is not stagnant. It moves and shifts and changes. The narrative style traces the action or chain of events in what Lowery calls the "homiletical plot." "Plot" means something related to the action in continuum. Not "point one, point two, point three" but "this" then "that" and "next." It includes both vocal and physical animation.

Action is followed by *tone*. For Lowery, tone "refers to the work's created subjective presence – the world view that stands silently articulated behind the writing."[13] Tone discloses the values and judgements within the narrative and allows both the proclaimer and the listener to establish a base for their individual judgement.

Finally, in the preliminary section, there is *narrative time*. This is not chronos of the watch but chronos of the spirit – the event medium in which the characters move and live. Of these elements Enslinger writes about Lowery's approach: "When a storyteller invites us into a 'world' with its setting, characters, action, and tone, narrative time is also begun. It is the time of the story."[14]

Lowery defines the process of the *sermon plot* in five stages: (1) upsetting the equilibrium, (2) analyzing the discrepancy, (3) disclosing the clue to resolution, (4) experiencing the gospel, and (5) anticipating the consequences.[15]

Upsetting the equilibrium is similar to the opening of a play, which sets the context for what is about to happen. In the introductory moment of a sermon, the preacher/proclaimer must establish the criteria of tension. What is so important in this text that the listener is willing to lay aside life to listen? Lowery suggests, "While the resolution of the plot should never be disclosed here, some direction to the ambiguity should be provided."[16]

Analyzing the discrepancy is stage two of the plot process. The preacher must not move too quickly to resolve; he or she must take the time to wrestle with the text. The what's and why's must be examined and theologized. In this diagnostic wrestling, one seeks to "uncover the areas of interior motivations where the problem is generated and hence expose the motivational setting toward which any cure will need be directed."[17]

Stage three is *disclosing the clue to resolution*. The preacher/proclaimer begins to shift to a point of resolution and toward a sense of outcome. As Craddock calls the preacher/proclaimer to reach the *eureka* point, Lowery says the congregation should also reach an *ah ha* moment when they are awakened to the clues which move to resolution.

The *ah ha* leads to step four, *experiencing the gospel*. Lowery says, "When I have done my diagnostic homework and the decisive clue has emerged, the good news has fallen into place sermonically as though pulled by a magnet."[18] With the realization of the gospel, the listener is led to the final stage - *anticipating the consequences*. In other words, what am I being asked to do? Lowery is quick to point out that the real decision of the listener is how the gospel applies to him or her personally comes in stage four. He says the focus of our preaching should be "upon the decisive activity of God, not upon us, and hence the climax of any sermon must be stage four – the experiencing of grace through the gospel."[19]

The actual presentation of the sermon in Lowery's methodology is not linear or pointed but resembles a story or narrative event. He says, "All preaching becomes an ordering of time into narrative time, the time of *our* story and *the* story,"[20] and it is the "*our* story and *the* story" concept which draws Lowery's methodology into my concept of Gospeltelling. Sermons should not be so much a telling of what one should or should not do but rather an invitation to join the journey towards an understanding and connection to/with the gospel story.

Eugene Lowery - Sermonic Plot

Aspects of Developing a Narrative Style	The Process of the Sermonic Plot
» Define the Setting » Identify the Characters » Locate the Action » Determine the Tone	» Upsetting the Equilibrium » Analyzing the Discrepancy » Disclosing the Clue to Resolution » Experiencing the Gospel » Anticipating the Consequences

Charles Rice - Preaching as Story

This "our story-God's story" concept is deepened in the use of story as sermon. Dr. Charles L. Rice, Professor Emeritus of Homiletics at Drew University, says, "If the Word is to become flesh in the event of preaching, a new approach to Scripture is necessary. Preaching must become more biblical, but not in the sense of proliferating Bible quotes, or intensifying the use of proof texts. ... the Story of God's self-disclosure is presented in specific stories about concrete human experience."[21] Rice lifts up storytelling as the "hermeneutical key," the understanding of Bible. In the story we find both understanding of the past and instruction for the present. Rices says that "when the minister who has ferried between tradition and experience stands before the congregation, it is as a storyteller that he or she communicates the Word."[22]

In this field of storytelling, I made my first firm stand to defend my style and my approach to proclamation. In the defense of the authentic "word," I made a textual stand. If someone is going to say, "The Bible says," then that person must be sure that is what the Bible says. The text/story is worthless unless it is able to touch lives with authenticity and authority. I have been like the nippy little dog at the heels of those who work in story. Tom Boomershine, Richard Ward, and Jay O'Callahan are some who may have grown weary of my questioning and query and yet have been faithful in sharing the craft and resources of storytelling. I continue to seek their wisdom because I have experienced the connectedness that comes when preacher, congregation, and Spirit find each other on common ground through the medium of story.

Rice notes the same experience: "The purpose of preaching is to enter into a shared story with the community of faith. Without that shared story, the basis for Christian life together is eroded; 'an acute sense of brokenness, unreality, and frustration ensues.'"[23] He continues, "Sermons which are born from an intimate relationship with Scripture and experience will derive their style and shape from inside the framework of a homiletical model of storytelling."[24]

Rice's metaphorical perspective challenges the preacher/proclaimer to approach the sermon in a three-fold fashion. First, he says to *let the metaphor interpret the metaphor without explanation*. There are times when we can say too much about something simple. Most have had the experience of trying to tell a joke or funny story only to see blank stares and puzzled looks. Struggling to recover, we begin to "explain" the joke or story, only to find ourselves wading into deeper waters of despair. Tex Sample, Professor of Church and Society at Saint Paul School of Theology, echoes this thought in his book <u>The Spectacle of Worship in a Wired World</u>: "Any oral person knows that the worse thing you can do is explain a story."[25] Sometimes the best thing to do is simply to walk away and try again later. If it needs to be explained the power of metaphor is lost.

Second of Rice's challenges is to *allow interplay between the lesson/text and the metaphor*. In Rice's methodology "the contemporary situation offers an issue or image which is then expanded and related to the biblical witness."[26]

Third, *one should derive the primary metaphor from the Bible itself.* When the preacher/proclaimer offers the congregation the biblical text, the listeners understand this is the core from which all other thoughts will emit. If the primary metaphor is not a part of the text, there is crisis on the part of the listener who wrestles with the connection between Word and word. Rice says that the Bible is itself a book of imagination where "language and stories can be experienced with power and feeling."[27]

The sermon may take many shapes in a storytelling form. There are times when the biblical story is self-explanatory and should be experienced as such. I am constantly reminded of how we as ministers have failed the congregation as biblical educators. Once, when I realized the only story most people knew about the Genesis character Joseph was something about a coat of many colors, I used as a sermon the entire Joseph story. Beginning with Genesis Chapter 37 and going through Chapter 50, the narrative storytelling provided for those people an image of one who did not remain a boy in a rainbow coat but, through the marvelous weavings of God's intervention and grace, became a very powerful and wise man – the very preserver/protector of the chosen people.

Sometimes the sermon may take the form of a personal story or the story of another person. Rice and I agree that in these sermons one must still return to the biblical metaphor or else it is just a good story.

Rice challenges us by saying, "What we look for in homiletics today are forms for the gospel that derive from what the gospel is, how it is communicated, and what God in Christ intends for our specific human communities."[28] The storytelling style of preaching can be energizing and creative. We can spread our imaginative wings and paint beautiful pictures which create for the listener images and vision, but if that is all they are, just images and visions, that is all they are. What sets the church apart from any other civic group is the spiritual connection, the God presence, the challenge to become spiritually alive. Our goal must be to make God and God's intention for our lives real. Rice puts it this way: "There is a need for sermons to be 'honed' and 'disciplined.' In short, the preacher who aims at nothing hits it."[29]

Charles Rice - Preaching as Story

Three-Fold Approach to Sermon as Story
1. Let the metaphor interpret the metaphor without explanation.   2. Allow interplay between the lesson/text and the metaphor.   3. Derive the primary metaphor from the Bible itself.

Henry Mitchell - Black Preaching

In the shifting sensorium of preaching, we have experienced the deliberate construction of a sermon, the fluid narrative style, and preaching as story. A cultural shift occurs when we move from the Anglo-Protestant venue to that of the Black Church. Dr. Henry H. Mitchell, who has served as Dean and Professor of History and Homiletics at the School of Theology at Virginia Union University, says, "The dullness of most mainline preaching is due to its being conceived of as argument rather than art – as syllogism rather than symbol."[30]

Growing up in the southern United States, I have been exposed to differing elements of black preaching. My first experience was as a child seeing a black preacher who went to the Courthouse Square every Saturday afternoon to do his stump-preaching. Dressed in his black suit, white shirt, and thin black tie, he loudly proclaimed his message while waving his large floppy Bible in the air. I do not remember any of his message, but I do remember how those walking up and down the sidewalks worked very hard at ignoring him.

My second experience was at a funeral. My father and mother worked outside the home. Beginning in my early years and extending into adulthood, a black lady by the name of Lula Mae Brown worked in my parent's home. She was cook, cleaner, disciplinarian, counselor, and, most of all, one who took care of the three siblings as if we were her own children. At Lula's funeral I found myself surrounded by a new experience. My parents and sister and brother were out of town when the funeral was scheduled. I was one of only two white faces in the congregation. (The other was the mayor of the city who seemed to attend every funeral in town whether he knew the person or not.) The service did not march through a liturgy and order but seemed to dance to a rhythmic beat that embraced those who came to celebrate a life and worship the God of life. The preacher, in his deep thundering voice, used Psalm 23 from the King James Version with all its majesty and poetic language. At this transition from the world of mortality into the realm of immortality, he reminded us that the psalmist said, "Yea, though I walk <u>through</u> the valley of the shadow of death – not around it, not under or over it, not stopping to stay in it, but through the valley!" And with his words of comfort and encouragement came the antiphonal cries of the congregation, encouraging the preacher to carry them on through the valley.

A critical shift came while I was doing work on my Doctor of Ministry degree at United Theological Seminary. We were divided into peer groups which centered on specific areas of work, and among the groups were three larger peer groups of black students. When we gathered for our intensives, some of their mentors preached the worship services, including Dr. Samuel D. Proctor and Dr. Henry H. Mitchell. Their sermons were powerful – I think! When we gathered in the chapel, all the black students sat up front and the rest of us gathered behind them. Once the preacher started his sermon, the antiphonal cries rose up from the floor. Their two-sided conversation was foreign to those of us brought up in white, Protestant churches. I had a hard time following the sermon because I experienced the interaction as noise. "If those down front would be quiet, I am sure this would be a powerful sermon," I said. Later I came to realize the power was not in a single voice but in the collective experience of worship.

Henry Mitchell describes the personal nature of black preaching as being relational: "Preaching must relate to the content as well as experience, and most especially to the deepest needs and longings of a person. 'Deep must call unto deep – personal depth speaking to personal depth.'"[31] In his book <u>Black Preaching</u>, he stresses the need for the gospel to be declared in the language and culture of those listening – a true vernacular. He defined the hermeneutic of such preaching as "putting the gospel on a tell-it-like-it-is, nitty-gritty basis."[32]

He describes preaching as an art dependent on the artist. The preacher/proclaimer must become interpreter of the biblical saga. He or she must be the eyewitness describing the external and internal dynamics of the story. As Mitchell says, "Immediacy and vividness are needed for such eyewitness accounts, and the preacher's challenge is to recount and/or elaborate the story in such a way that it can be relived today."[33]

Mitchell speaks of the process of black preaching by establishing four criteria for the event. First, *the preacher must become the "gatekeeper,"* who monitors the information and emotion of the experience. Second is *the preacher's sensitivity to timing,* not clock timing but spirit timing. Gardner C. Taylor says, "Emotion takes time." As in Lowery's concept of the revelation of the climax, Mitchell says the climax cannot be disclosed too soon or else the element of celebration will be lost: "While the sermon may move the hearers along a number of hills and valleys, the expectation is always that at last the journey will conclude on the mountain top."[34]

The third element is that of *dialog.* Black preaching is antiphonal in that it calls for the congregation to become involved in the sermonic process. Mitchell illustrates this when he says, "The Black worshipper does not merely acknowledge the Word delivered by the preacher; he talks back! Sometimes the Black worshipper may shout."[35] In large part, the success of black preaching comes from the knowledge of the congregation. During some of the chapel services, the preacher started into a text or biblical story, and, as he began the sentence or passage, the congregation finished the thought for the preacher. The "white" church is still trying to figure out the story while the black church already knows the story and is willing to offer their assistance as they, the listeners and the preacher, join together in the journey.

The fourth element is *the dimensions of free expression and self-disclosure.* Taking this risk, the preacher becomes part therapist. Mitchell says: "In a hostile white world, they have had to be close-lipped and poker-faced to survive. . . . . There must be a place where Blacks can actually open up and let out feelings safely."[36] I have often heard the expression that 11:00 a.m. on Sunday morning is the most segregated hour on earth, but that cannot be dismissed as simply a racial bias. It has to do with why a person goes to church and what he or she expects to receive and carry away. For most "white" churches, the feeling is to receive knowledge and wisdom. In the black church, it is to experience release and healing of the spirit. Mitchell says that maybe the black church has a balm the American white person does not know about.

Several years ago an elderly woman in my congregation approached me one Sunday morning and said, "I have had this book for years and I want to pass it on to you." The small book with the golden cover was indeed a treasure. It was the 1938 edition of James Weldon Johnson's <u>God's Trombones: Seven Negro Sermons In Verse</u>. The poems/sermons illustrate how the black preachers draw the biblical story into their story. From the ancient text they recast the image so it is their image.

In the poem "The Creation," Weldon uses the illusion that God is like a black mother:

> Up from the bed of the river
> God scooped up the clay;
> And by the bank of the river
> He kneeled down;
> And there the great God Almighty
> Who lit the sun and fixed it in the sky
> Who flung the stars to the most far corner of the night,
> Who rounded the earth in the middle of his hand;
> This Great God,
> Like a mammy bending over her baby,
> Kneeled down in the dust
> Toiling over a lump of clay
> Till he shaped it in his own image;
> Then into it he blew the breath of life, And man became a living soul.[37]

Weldon also uses the metaphor of Babylon as the far country in his poem about the prodigal son. I heard a sermon preached by a black preacher who said the prodigal son came riding into the far country in his pink Cadillac. Samuel Proctor, as he preached a sermon on our relationship with God, drew his sermon to a close talking about his desire to be with God. He would go out into the lonely, dark places and call on God's name. He continued as he described how God would come and be with him and comfort him and how God would walk and talk with him. Suddenly the listeners realize they are in the middle of a song:

> *"I come to the garden alone while the dew is still on the roses,*
> *And the voice I hear falling on my ear,*

The Son of God discloses.
And he walks with me and he talks with me.
And he tells me I am his own. ... "[38]

The black preaching sensorium is multilevel. It moves from the heart-felt experience of the preacher and is echoed in the affirmation of the listener. It calls forth to make a journey, and the people are willing to come along. It is narrative, emotional, and experiential. It is here, for me, the proclamation moment begins to move from preaching to Gospeltelling.

Several years ago there were several bumper stickers which addressed the issue of perspective. "You wouldn't understand – it's a _____ thing!" The words filling the blank varied: it's a male thing; it's a female thing; it's a Southern thing; it's a black thing; it's a Native American thing! These mini-billboards called us to be aware of perspective. No two people stand in the same place or have exactly the same experiences. Along with that, cultures and gender make a difference in how we perceive differing stimuli. This is particularly true in the church as more and more pulpits and chancels are being filled with persons of differing gender and ethnicity. A saying attributed to the Native Americans points us in the right direction: "Before you criticize others walk a mile in their shoes (moccasins)." We have walked in several pairs of homiletical shoes and now we turn to another pair – the feminine perspective.

Henry Mitchell - A Black Approach to Preaching

Criteria for the Preaching Event
1. The preacher must become the "gatekeeper" of information and emotion.
2. The preacher must be sensitive to timing – spiritual timing.
3. The preacher must be open to dialog with the listener.
4. The preacher must have the dimensions of free expression and self-disclosure.

Patricia Wilson-Kastner – Preaching as a Single Image

O.C. Edwards calls attention to a survey conducted at a conference on "Women and Preaching." The survey was used to differentiate the perceptions in preaching. The results are as follows *(see figure on next page)*:

PERCEIVED GENDER DIFFERENCES IN PREACHING

M ale	1980	Female
	Content	
Intellectual		Down-to-earth
Theological		Emotional
Jargon		Personal
Hard questions		Experiential
Abstract		Life issues
Traditional and		No point
male illustrations		Too personal
	Delivery	
Confident		Solicitous
Controlled		Inviting
Voice-rich		Apologetic
Strong		Hesitant
Bigger		Animated
		Hard to hear
		Expressive
		Warm
	Style	
Formal		Informal
Forceful		Warm
Rational		Personal
Organized		Apologetic
Authoritarian		Ingratiating
Remote		[39]

At first glance we move into a comparative format. The left side of the chart responds one way while the other side of the chart responds with another action. However, if one skews the isolating focus, one can experience the complementary attributes of the differences between the male and female approaches to preaching. It became a joke as men were challenged to get in touch with their feminine side, but we must remember that we do not preach to segregated congregations. If the preacher/proclaimer wishes to proclaim the gospel message to "all" the people, then he or she must approach that moment with a sensitivity to the differing characteristics of those listening.

The survey taken in 1980 was re-addressed in 1994 with this general response: "Women's preaching is described in more positive, receptive tones and words than in the earlier study. . . . Hearers appear to register a stronger feeling response to women preaching than to men."[40] I think this statement is born out in the number of women filling our pulpits and their success as preacher/pastor. We only have to surf the religious stations on the television to see the ever-increasing presence of women who have risen to prominence and power within the media.

With this sensitivity, we turn to hear the voice of Patricia Wilson-Kastner. Dr. Wilson-Kastner was the Trinity Church Professor of Preaching at General Theological Seminary in New York City. Using the elements of the female side of the survey, Wilson-Kastner embraced the down-to-earth, emotional, experiencial attributes and moved us from a broadness of narrative to a focus on image – a single image.

In her book <u>Imagery for Preaching</u>, Dr. Wilson-Kastner dismisses the trivial use of imagery:

> Images are not just a gimmick to attract people before giving them solid doctrine. Images are not candy, while abstractions are meat. Today's preacher lives in a world that is steadily moving in its appraisal of human nature toward a balance of the intellectual and the emotional, the rational and the intuitive. ... If preachers hope to communicate effectively with congregations, then we ignore this new emphasis on image and imagery at our peril.[41]

She challenges us to look beyond the old norms of homiletical process and embrace imagery as a central focus of communicating the gospel: "Imagery is a more encompassing term than images. Imagery is defined by one editorial team as 'the sensory quality of a literary work.' Imagery means more than pictures; it includes the whole physical and sensory dimension of the world portrayed in a sermon."[42] It is this sensory experience I have defined as the Gospeltelling Sensorium.

Wilson-Kastner suggests that in the development process, one seeks a single image to be the central focus. This does not mean other images are abandoned; they are used to support or clarify the primary image. The image chosen may rise from the dust of the ancient text or spring forward from contemporary life. The image should be suggested by the biblical text/material on which the sermon is based. Wilson-Kastner says that "the first step, of course, is prayerfully and thoughtfully to explore the Scripture readings assigned for the service of which the sermon is a part."[43]

In the process of developing the "image," Wilson-Kastner offers a list of nuances which may be used in seeking the appropriate image. First, is the image *congruent*? She says, "The imagery of the sermon needs to be consistent with and expressive of the religious experience, ideas, and feelings to be conveyed."[44] If the text speaks about the "Light of Christ," the concept is simple and has a variety of images easily associated with that theme. One would not want to use the image of a ship or a rock because it would not be congruent with the text and would only lead to the confusion for the listener.

The second nuance is that of *commonality:* "The most effective imagery in preaching is directly and immediately familiar to the hearer."[45] In the season of Lent, we hear Jesus' lament over Jerusalem, and he uses the image of a mother hen gathering her chicks beneath her wings, but how many people in the twenty-first century are eyewitnesses to that common barnyard event? Wilson-Kastner is quick to point out that many of the biblical images are not common to those listening to the text and suggests, "The preacher may choose to select a contemporary image serving some of the same functions for us as a corresponding image in biblical times."[46]

In 1987, I was driving from my home to my brother's home in Georgia for a visit. The trip carried me through a rural area of West Alabama, where agriculture continues to be primary in the economy. To my surprise, I passed a field where a man was plowing with a mule. I quickly returned to my childhood, remembering when my father hired an older man to bring his mule and plow our backyard garden every spring. To watch that man unhitch the mule from his wagon and harness up the plow, to hear him whistle and call out directions as he dug the plow into the soil, to experience the scent of moist dirt rising to the surface – these are real images for me. Watching that man in the field not only brought back those memories but also placed me in the reflective state saying, "If only my children could see this." They have never seen a man plowing. They have never heard the whistle or call. To plow a straight furrow means nothing to them. What image could I use which would carry the commonality? Maybe they would relate to holding to the handles of a lawnmower as they try to cut the grass in straight lines.

Multidimensionality is the next nuance and is illustrated by images which carry or can sustain many meanings. Two elements must be addressed. First, does the image have the capacity to communicate various dimensions of the human person? Second, can this image carry with it new meanings which can be experienced when couched in a single image? WilsonKastner illustrates as follows:

> If the preacher starts a sermon by acclaiming God as a rock, then the congregation needs to see the rock. Is it a big rock, or a pebble? Is it a strong rock, a boulder in the field, or does it rise unexpectedly and overwhelmingly from the yellow plains of the desert? Is the rock massive, smooth, and worn, a shelter from the heat of the sun and a wall to lean against, or is it steep and sharp, hard to climb because it trips and tears you, but offers the safety of Mesada when you have climbed it? The congregation should feel the unyielding power of the rock, the heat of the sun reflecting off it, and rejoice in its protective height. . . . The preacher needs to lead the congregation on this sort of verbal sensory journey. If our senses are not fully active and involved so that the image becomes a vital part of our reality, then nothing else of the sermon will remain with us either.[47]

Then there is *appeal:* "Appeal does not necessarily mean like or agree with, but appeal does involve immediate identification with some aspect or quality that I am happy, ready, or able to find in myself."[48] This then leads to the final nuance which asks if the image is *open-ended:* "One of the joys of a good image is that it always has more grace and truth hiding in it, ready to emerge to meet us when we seek for it. . . . A good image contains unending potential for God's revealing Word to be known to us. No matter how often we preach on or consider it, the image always bears more riches."[49]

Wilson-Kastner's nuances tell us what image should do. Then comes the decision on what image to use. She suggests five questions to use in assessing an image:

1. What is the root of this image in common human experiences?
2. How does this image portray God?
3. What does this image imply about God's relationship to human beings?
4. What response to God does this image evoke in the hearer?
5. How is this image complimented by other images?[50]

As with Craddock's "single statement" which drives the sermon, so a single image can represent that statement as the foundation of a sermon, but that image must be relative and appropriate.

Patricia Wilson-Kastner - Single Image

The Nuances of Developing the Image
1. The image must be congruent.
2. The image must process commonality.
3. The image must be multidimensional.
4. The image must be open-ended.

Thomas Troeger - Imagining the Sermon

"God does not conquer by force but by capturing the imagination." Spoken by Thomas Troeger, these words echoed in the small auditorium at Camp Sumatanga, a United Methodist Retreat Center in North Alabama. Dr. Thomas H. Troeger is the

Ralph E. and Norma E. Peck Professor of Preaching and Communications at Illiff School of Theology in Denver, Colorado. A talented musician, Troeger called the sessions together by playing his flute and then asked a very powerful question: "Preacher, what do you see?" In his book <u>Imagining A Sermon</u>, Troeger challenges us to get our heads out of the book and lift them into the clouds. His work compliments Patricia Wilson-Kastner in imagery, placing the work of an artist next to and with the task of the preacher.

Troeger calls for a shift from the classical rhetorical pattern. He lists the seven tasks of rhetoric: 1) clarity of the argument; 2) logic of the outline; 3) tightness of the transitions; 4) development of the main point; 5) persuasiveness of the reasoning; 6) appropriateness of the illustrations to the principles; and 7) the theological defensibility of the message.[51]   In response he offers seven principles for the practice of imaginative theology: 1) alert the eye to keener sight; 2) feel the bodily weight of the truth; 3) listen to the music of speech; 4) draw parables from life; 5) understand the church's resistance to imagination; 6) dream of new worlds; and 7) return to the source.[52] All of these principles re-address his earlier question now recast from the front side of the chancel: "Can the listener see your sermon?"

Troeger's book is an expansion of the seven principles. I will not define each principle, but I will share the statements which can challenge us to reevaluate not only how we think about sermon but also how we will preach/proclaim the gospel message.

Troeger challenges us to become more visual by asking some imagining questions: "Where is the road? Where is the mountain? Where is the light? Where is the crowd? How will one's gestures and glances suggest the location of these things to the congregation?"[53] With the answers to these questions came the memory of what Dr. Richard Ward taught me as a student in storytelling at Chandler School of Theology in Atlanta. He said that when imagining a scene, place objects and then keep them there. If the mountain is to the left, then every time the teller looks to the mountain, he or she looks left.

Along with the placement of image comes the feel of image: "Whether joyful or saddening, truth that matters has a bodily weight, a physical force on our animal frames. This should come as no surprise to Christians, who believe that 'the Word became flesh,' not a cloud or a thought but flesh, a human being."[54]   There is indeed a major difference between "telling/speaking" feeling and the "showing/exhibiting" feeling. If the text speaks of anger, the teller should be angry. If the story tells of sadness, he or she should be sad.

He also addresses the changing culture: "Before we can preach those sacred visions effectively, we need to understand how our listeners imagine the world. They do not live in biblical times or reformation times or even modern times. They live in the postmodern, mass media age that has conditioned them to perceive and experience the world in new ways."[55] Even though we preach to as many as four generations on Sunday morning, each experiencing life in differing arenas, they all live in the here-and-now. The images we use must be multigenerational, multi-cultural, and relevant.

Finally, Troeger challenges us to return to the Source. What Craddock calls *eureka*, and some call the *ah ha* moment, he moves to that "be still and know" moment as we listen for the sighs of the Spirit. "In listening to the sighs of the Spirit, we receive power to do what is good and just and right. And when preachers attend to the sighs of the Spirit, their words take on the quality of heaven's voice, and their speaking awakens in the listeners an awareness of the Spirit sighing within them," he said at the conference. He illustrates this focus in his poem "Center on Christ Alone:"

> Heart, hold fast, one truth clasp:
> Center on Christ alone.
>
> Mind, be still, do God's will:
> Center on Christ alone.
>
> Soul, drive deep, one thought keep:
> Center on Christ alone. On Christ alone.
>
> Church, bow low, one faith know:
> Center on Christ alone. On Christ alone.
>
> World, draw near, one word hear:
> Center on Christ alone.
> On Christ alone.
> Christ alone.
> Christ.[56]

Thomas Troeger - Imagining the Sermon

Three-Fold Approach to Sermon as Story
1. Alert the eye to keener sight.   2. Feel the bodily weight of the truth.   3. Listen to the music of speech.   4. Draw parables from life.   5. Understand the church's resistance to imagination   6. Dream of new worlds   7. Return to the Source

We have made this exploratory journey almost complete. We have heard Craddock speak of an inductive method of proclamation. We have marched through Eugene Lowery's sermonic plot. We shifted gears as we entered the sermon as story by Charles Rice. We were cast deeper into experiential telling as Henry Mitchell offered the image of the black preacher. Patricia Wilson-Kastner offered a dual role of preaching from a feminine perspective and from the point of a single image. Thomas Troeger broadened our vision by calling us to dream.

Each style and process is valuable as we experience the proclamation sensorium, but as I made this personal journey to evaluate my own style and preference, I was reminded of the words that Fred Craddock, Thomas Troeger, and others have echoed. The more a person thinks that he or she has discovered a new and unique approach to the homiletical/rhetorical process the more he or she realize that the new concept is nothing more than an ornamentation of the ancient standards.

Before I close, let me address a new element in proclamation – multimedia. As I have observed, the preaching styles and concepts have changed very little in this Postmodern/Digital age. Some still preach on the basis of the three part epideictic style – introduction, body, and conclusion. There are those who preach thematically, grasping at any verse which can be authentically or randomly attached to a central thought. Others preach in an expository style of verse by verse, as others tell the message through image and story.

Tex Sample reminds us that, even though we find ourselves in a multimedia age, we continue to be primarily an oral culture. We do not sit in silent worship. We do not offer only a PowerPoint slide to present the gospel message. We live and worship in a world of sight and sound. The Word of God must be presented in a manner that can be heard and absorbed by the current culture. Sample says, "Let me begin with a truism. What you cannot remember in an oral culture you do not know."[57] We know by two avenues. The first is personal experience. The second is listening to the experience of others. Sample illustrates this by referring to a conversation between Sam Mann, a white preacher, and a black parishioner of the church where he was a guest preacher. He had preached what he thought to be a powerful sermon on his view of Christogy. After the service this parishioner, who was seventy-eight years old, grabbed the sleeve of his robe and waving her finger in his face said, "Reverend Mann, Reverend Mann, I did not come to this church to hear what somebody else said *about* Jesus. I came to hear what *Jesus* said to *you!*"[58] This drives home what many of the leading preachers remind us. If we, who are called to bring the message of Christ to others, do not have a relationship with the Christ we proclaim, our message is void of truth. We must, whichever approach we use as a proclamation pattern, make that message relate to those who gather to hear God's word *to them.*

Multimedia has greatly influenced the sensorium of worship. We do not enter a brightly colored sanctuary but rather a dim theater. We no longer bury our heads in the hymnal when we sing but look up at a screen for words. We no longer vibrate with the deep, low tones of the pipe organ but bounce to the rhythm of drums, guitars, and tambourines. This is not to say that those "traditional" styles have disappeared, for they have not and probably outnumber those termed "contemporary," but people are flocking to this new worship experience, which includes, as was included in the early church, a time of proclamation.

Now that time of proclamation has a new dimension. The media screen has become an integral part of worship and preaching. Some preachers use the screen to list the points and themes of their sermons. Some may use it as a place for showing pictures and images to illustrate a point or thought. Others use live video to present the preachers in larger-than-life fashion so the listeners can see the fire in their eyes and steam from their nostrils. But even with this technology, the proclamation moment remains what it has been for years – only painted with slightly different hues.

Chapter 3 Endnotes

1. Craddock, <u>Preaching</u>, 24.
2. Craddock, <u>As One Without Authority</u>, 57.
3. Craddock
4. Craddock, <u>Preaching</u>, 105.
5. Craddock, 110 - 111.
6. Craddock, 118-119.
7. Craddock, 138.
8. Craddock, 141.
9. Craddock, 147-148.
10. Craddock, 183.
11. Craddock, 216.
12. Eslinger, <u>A New Hearing</u>, 65.
13. Eslinger, 74.
14. Eslinger.
15. Eslinger, 78.
16. Eslinger, 79.
17. Eslinger, 80.
18. Eslinger, 82.
19. Eslinger, 83.
20. Eslinger, 84.
21. Eslinger, 19.
22. Eslinger, 23.
23. Eslinger, 24.
24. Eslinger, 26.
25. Sample, <u>The Spectacle of Worship in a Wired World</u>, 13.
26. Eslinger, 26.
27. Eslinger, 28.
28. Eslinger, 25.
29. Eslinger.
30. Eslinger, 39.
31. Eslinger, 40.
32. Mitchell, <u>Black Preaching</u>, 30.
33. Eslinger, 46.
34. Eslinger, 47.
35. Mitchell, 44.
36. Mitchell, 111.
37. Johnson, <u>God's Trombones</u>, 20.
38. C. Austin Miles, *In The Garden*, 1913.

39. Edwards, 752.
40. Edwards, 753.
41. Wilson-Kastner, <u>Imagery for Preaching</u>, 17.
42. Wilson-Kastner, 20.
43. Wilson-Kastner, 50.
44. Wilson-Kastner, 51.
45. Wilson-Kastner, 53.
46. Wilson-Kastner, 54.
47. Wilson-Kastner, 55.
48. Wilson-Kastner, 59.
49. Wilson-Kastner.
50. Edwards, 818.
51. Troeger, <u>Imagining A Sermon</u>, 29.
52. Troeger, 29-30.
53. Troeger, 35.
54. Troeger, 53.
55. Troeger, 120.
56. Thomas Troeger, *Center on Christ*, presented to the Bishop's Convocation on Ministry.
57. Sample, <u>Ministry in an Oral Culture</u>, 13.
58. Sample, 73.

Chapter 4
Gospeltelling to a Digital Culture

In 1991 Steven Spielberg produced a film titled *Hook*[1] based on the fictional character Peter Pan. Peter has grown up and forgotten his Neverland adventures. He has become Peter Banner, a high-powered lawyer who has let the business world control his life even to the expense of the caretaking of his own children. Two scenes stirred my imagination as they speak to the issues of proclamation/sermon.

The first scene opens with Peter and his family returning to England. Granny Wendy, when seeing how preoccupied Peter seems, asks, "And what is so terribly important about your terribly important business?" Jack, Peter's son, quickly fires a response, "Well, you see, when a big company is in trouble, Dad sails in, and, if there is any resistance, he just blows them out of the water!" Lifting her eyes in a wondering fashion, she replies, "So, Peter, you have become a pirate!"

After his children are captured by Captain Hook, Peter returns to Neverland but does not remember his adventures there. The Lost Boys become skeptical at the insistence that this "grown-up" is the famous Peter Pan. He does not look like the boy wonder who left so many years before. He does not sound nor act like the famous Peter Pan, who could crow like a rooster and fly. Lost in a sense of despair, Peter falls to his knees. A small boy walks up to the kneeling Peter and begins to massage his face. He stretches Peter's face up and down and then tightly back from each side. Suddenly his eyes light up as he exclaims, "Oh, there you are, Peter!"

We can approach the proclamation moment in two ways. We can hoist the sails of the text and proclaim our view in such a way that anyone who differs with our opinion will fear getting "blown out of the water." Or, we can stretch, explore, and massage the text until God reveals the truth to be proclaimed.

The forensic reconstruction of a story requires the careful examination of a text, which sometimes requires us to look below the surface for a new or appropriate message. The process I call Gospeltelling is a model by which we dig deep into the ancient text;

immerse ourselves in the culture, words, and spirit of the text; and then exit into the world of the Digital Culture declaring, "This is what it says to us today." The danger here is making the Bible a clearinghouse for metaphors or nonchalant illustrations. We must be conscious not to force a metaphor or image, created simply to prove our point, not the particular point of the pericope.

In an email newsletter from a provider of contemporary worship materials, the subject concerned the image the worship team had conceived as the metaphor for the service and the biblical verses or the text used for the proclamation. In reality the two were incongruent. One side, either the worship team or the preacher/proclaimer, would be required to shift focus. The ensuing discussion exposed the struggle of the pastor to grasp the image/metaphor as it did not fit his interpretation of the scripture passage. The doggedness of the "team" eventually weakened the pastor to submission. He then felt forced to adjust the textual concept to comply with the metaphor selected by the team. It was the round peg in a square hole episode. I was not privy to the worship event nor the dynamics of what experience was born out of this dilemma. My feeling is that it would be manifested in one of two areas. In the first, all eventually worked together for a presenting and understanding of the metaphor. In the second, the listener would grasp the metaphor of worship but struggle to find the connection with the sermon/proclamation.

The worship experience, especially in a contemporary setting where teams of persons work together to develop concepts, images, and metaphors, can be affected by the approach to its creation. A team can either select the metaphor and force everything into its image with the challenge of "blow them out of the water!" or the entire team – music, drama, graphics, messenger – can jointly massage the entirety of the experience until, out of the tugging and shifting of thought, there arises the surprising exclamation "Oh, there you are!"

Gospeltelling is an epideictic rhetorical process which forms itself into a three-fold proclamation event. The introduction (setting the stage), the body (examining the story), and the conclusion (the answer to the "so what" question) are the components of the final production. Even though I do not see this as a "narrative sermon," it has a narrative/storytelling texture. This oral pattern recognizes that the event is not to be a cranial but rather an experiential encounter.

Len Wilson and Jason Moore's book <u>Digital Storytellers: The Art of Communicating the Gospel in Worship</u> broadens the concept of narrative form to encompass the entire worship experience: "A narrative approach to worship gives a holistic picture of the Gospel, which goes beyond a lesson-on-the-day mentality that focuses on behavior modification, to a deeper understanding of who we are in Christ."[2]

If one simply tells the message in an inviting manner rather than forcing or preaching at the congregation, those listening will join on the journey rather than hop off the train at its first stop. The entire process is a six-part journey, which expresses itself in the steps of (1) selecting the text, (2) experiencing the text, (3) exploring the text, (4) bridging the text, (5) imaging the text, and (6) proclaiming the text.

Gospeltelling Journey
1)   Selecting the Text
    2)   Experiencing the Text
        3)   Exploring the Text
            4)   Bridging the Text
                5)   Imaging the Text
                    6)   Proclaiming the Text

Selecting the Text

For the pastor/preacher/proclaimer, almost as soon as he or she steps away from the worship event on Sunday morning, the mind begins to wonder about what will be said or proclaimed in that same space next week. For some, the process has simplicity in the form of a predetermined scripture lesson using of the lectionary calendar. The three-year cycle not only offers a variety of Gospel texts and stories but also suggests an Old Testament text as well as a Psalm and a reading from a Letter or an Epistle. For others, who select their own text, it can be a constant struggle to create for themselves patterns and methods that allow for a variety of stories and themes.

As a child and youth, I worshiped in a church which did not use the lectionary. I remember a pastor who served my church for a number of years, who, in his words, "preached the entire Bible." Even as a young person, I recognized that the preacher had only a handful of sermons, slightly adjusted to make way for the reading of a different text.

Dr. Craddock, in my homiletics class, addressed this issue of text selection and challenged us to use the lectionary even when the text seems obscure. He said the mystery of the Gospel is its ability to speak to each generation. The task of the preacher/proclaimer is to embrace the text by asking the question "What is God wanting to say to us today?"

For the most part I use the lectionary pattern and primarily the Gospel lesson. It provides a structure for understanding the Christian year and also encompasses all four gospels. The Reverend John Fenton, Canon of Christ Church College, Oxford University, England, in his seminar on the Gospel of Matthew, brought me to an awareness of the shifting balance in the lectionary readings, which, in the early formation in the Anglican Church, as well as other traditions, held to the opinion that Matthew was the oldest of the Gospels. This resulted in the readings being weighed in Matthew's favor. Carl Lachmann (circa 1835) discovered that Mark was the oldest writing, and in response to this enlightenment, a shift came in the lectionary distribution of Gospel texts. As I compared the Prayer Book of 1662 with the more contemporary lectionaries, I found a more balanced approach to the four Gospel readings. The following chart illustrates how the more recent lectionaries offer a three-year journey, which covers the majority of the Gospel materials. All things considered, i.e. the size of the Gospel book itself and the way the weight of particular subject matter such as the birth narratives and passion narratives, the lectionary is a balanced approach to Gospel proclamation.

Gospel	Anglican Prayer Book of 1662	Prayer Book of Alternative Services 1980	Revised Common Lectionary 1992
Matthew	37%	24%	26%
Mark	4%	12%	17%
Luke	31%	27%	28.5%
John	28%	37%	28.5% [3]

If there is a fault I have with the lectionary readings, it is that they are void of much of the Old Testament story. I have deviated from the lectionary and have spend large blocks of time going through the Genesis stories and the stories of the Exodus. I have also enjoyed struggling with the books of Job and Jonah. These texts cannot be addressed in one proclamation or receive justification by extracting small units from the entire story but must be extended to a number of hearings to create an understanding for the dynamics of the story itself.

I have heard a number of my colleagues respond to the lectionary by saying that "I preach what God has placed on my heart from week to week." I bow to those who have that sensitivity, but I also have experienced some of those persons who seem to revisit the same material over and over again as did my former pastor.

Another issue is the type of text to use in a Gospeltelling motif. My process lends itself to the narrative sections of the Bible. For me it is hard to develop a narrative/conversational style of proclamation when attempting to address the dictates of Levitical law or Pauline chastisement. I am not saying it cannot be done – I am just saying it does not fit me. To address those texts, one could use another style or, as I have so often done, use those texts in a Bible Study setting. Here again I do not claim my methodology is the "correct" pattern but simply one of many. A person must find the proclamation style which is appropriate for his or her personal demeanor, theological beliefs, and contextual composition.

The text should propel us forward on our Christian journey not drive us toward guilt or spiritual anxiety. If any biblical texts have the ability to propel us forward for the sake of Christ, they are the pericopes in the four Gospels. The stories surrounding the life and teachings of Christ awaken in us the reality of our own lives, stir the emotion to social consciousness, and place us in the spotlight of self-examination. The alternative texts, especially some of the Pauline and Epistle writings, have a way of bringing a heavy burden of boundary and submission.

Clarence Jordan wrote an unique version of the Gospels titled <u>The Cotton Patch Gospels</u>. This retelling of the gospel story sets the biblical events in the American South. The city of Nazareth is now Gainesville, Georgia, and Jerusalem becomes Atlanta. The book was turned into a Broadway play and is still played by traveling theatrical groups and local community theaters. In the production, at a powerful point where the parable of the Good Samaritan is being taught, a large tour bus belonging to a "hot gospel quartet" arrives on the scene They exit the bus to sing one of the songs from their latest album. As applause roars through the theater, one of the quartet members seeks an encore by crying, "Do you want to hear the flip-side?"

There is a flip-side to this process. The process to this point is primarily a solo event. Michael Slaughter, in his book <u>Out on the Edge</u>, defines this approach as "lone-ranger mentality." He explains that

> In the modern industrial age, most contributions were made by entrepreneurs such as Ford, Edison, and Disney. In the post-modern world, there are no more Thomas Edisons. Great contributions are made through the collaborative efforts of teams. Teams are more effective and durable in the navigation of turbulent times. Ongoing collaborative relationships stimulate creativity and consistent exceptional performance.[4]

In the book <u>Emerging Worship</u>, Dan Kimball charts the differing approaches to worship planning as follows:

MODERN	**EMERGING**
The senior pastor determines what is taught in the worship service.	The lead pastor involves both the church community and the staff in determining what is taught in the worship gatherings.
The sermon is the center of the worship service – music and anything else are "extra."	The combination of many creative elements experienced in community points to Jesus as the centerpiece.
The senior pastor gives the worship leader direction for enhancing the sermon with music and other creative elements.	The worship team (including the lead pastor) direct the design of the worship gatherings.

-continued-

The weekend service team consists of the senior pastor and worship leader alone.	The weekend service team includes the teacher, the music leader, the artists, the photographers, the video and PowerPoint team, the sacred space team, etc.
Creativity causes stress to the pastors. They must always outdo what they did last time in order to please people.	Creativity causes relief and lack of stress as worship gatherings become more fluid, more naturally creative, thanks to the efforts of a team of people.[5]

In the new worship paradigm, teams design the entire worship event. I will not address the entire process of creating a worship service through the team effort here since there are so many good resources which help churches establish patterns for the worship event, but I will point out that in the new paradigm of the church, a collaborative effort defines the elements included in worship, and this effort includes the selection of the biblical text and theme of the sermon/proclamation.

Text selection then has opposing processes. On one side, the pastor/preacher/teacher makes all the significant decisions. On the other side, the text is selected in collaboration with an entire team. In the defense of the pastor/teacher, the way the text is selected is not always in his or her control. By way of example, the United Methodist Church has a "sent" clergy. Ministers are appointed to churches via the direction of the Bishop and Cabinet of each conference. Those who, in the past, have had the sole responsibility of text selection may suddenly find themselves as part of a team, and, as has been the case, one who has been part of a team process may be appointed to a church that wants the pastor to "do it all." Here, as in so many facets of ministry, one must be flexible.

Experiencing the Text

After the text is selected, the next issue is that of translation, which can be a very sensitive matter. Some churches/denominations have particular translations they sanction to be used in public worship. The first week of June is the traditional time for the North Alabama Conference of the United Methodist Church, of which I am an elder, to meet for its annual business session. During this time proposals are presented for the consideration of the conference. For years, and years, and years, a gentleman would present a document which asked the Annual Conference to make the 1611 King James Bible the only authorized bible to be used in the pulpits of the churches. He did allow the flexibility to use other translations in Bible Study and Sunday School Classes. The vote was always overwhelmingly against such a requirement, but it raises the question as to which text should be used.

The 1611 KJV language alienates the listener who dwells in a digital culture. A person who listens to that text today spends the entire reading trying to reinterpret the vocabulary. It is the same effect as when we listen to Shakespeare. We enjoy the imagery on the stage but struggle with the vocabulary of the actors. Many churches use a bible contemporary in its vocabulary. Of all the contemporary versions on the market, I prefer the <u>Contemporary English Version</u> (CEV), produced by the American Bible Society in 1995. In the late 1990's I was a presenter for the American Bible Society's regional meetings in Alabama and Georgia. At these meetings I visited with Dr. Barclay Newman, the catalist behind the translation, and inquired as to the nature of translation process. The National Bible Society describes the CEV as follows: "The goals of the translators of the CEV were to create a Bible version that could 'be read aloud without stumbling, heard without misunderstanding, and listened to with enjoyment and appreciation' and have a 'lucid and lyrical' style."[6]

Two things set this translation high on my list. The first reason I prefer the CEV is that it is indeed a literal translation. Newman said the process began with a word-for-word sequence translation from the original languages. When the translators completed a sentence, their first question would be "How do we say that today?" This would often require the sentence to be restructured, taking the last of the sentence and moving it to the front for clarity. Second, clarity of style lends itself to an oral event. The text reads aloud well and was translated with a cross-generational intent.

Another translation is the <u>New International Version</u> (NIV) published by the International Bible Society, which now includes the recently updated New Testament titled <u>Today's New International</u>

Version (TNIV), a more gender sensitive version. This quickly became the standard of many churches as this version replaced an archaic text with a more contemporary reading. This version is also a literal translation, and it uses contemporary language, which lends itself to good oral production. The translation process differs from the CEV in that the TNIV and NIV attempt to keep the sentence structure congruent with the original text.

The third translation, and the one I use the most, is the New Revised Standard Version (NRSV - Division of Christian Education of the National Council of the Churches of Christ in the United States of America). I do not think I would find many arguments against the statement that this is the most scholarly translation in the field. In an article published in the *Birmingham News* titled "Early Bible Translations Losing Popularity," Dr. Paul Holloway, Professor of Religion at Samford University, Birmingham, Alabama, points to the popularity of the NIV translation among the laity. Holloway categorizes the NIV as "a translation in which the emphasis is on theology, not scholarship." He says the NRSV is "a scholarly translation," and he uses this translation in the Religion Department at Samford.[7] The NRSV translation keeps the original sentence structure. The language is not "easy" but is comprehensible to those in the late teenage years and older. When I do text-critical work, I use the NRSV because I feel more connected to the original texts. This is a personal feeling, of course, but I do use the other texts in worship settings. Most frequently, I use the TNIV, and on occasion I use the CEV. The decision is made according to the fluidness of the reading and the perception of how the listeners will perceive the text.

No matter which translation one selects, the first thing to do is to read the text aloud. To read the text silently and then anticipate a grand response to the oral reading is ambitious. Very few persons can develop oral material in silence. Nothing sets a bad platform for the proclamation moment than to have it sound as if this is the first time one has read the scripture text. I can expand that thought by saying that when reading aloud, one should read the text while standing. In the standing and moving, one can experience the dynamics of the textual sound, textual rhythm, and textual movement. It is in a continuum of that process that I suggest reading the text to make it larger than life. Using exaggerated gestures and extreme vocal expensiveness (i.e.: pitch and tone variants) lends itself to the text disclosing itself. If there are different characters in the text one should give each a voice – then listen to the "voices."

Another way of experiencing the text is to rewrite the text in a different format. This is not original with me, and I do not know whom to credit. But I suggest writing the text in a column one word after another. It is time-consuming and awkward, but the process forces me to see the sentence structure become prominent in another format. Often words or phrases surface which would have been glossed over if they were in their traditional format. The prologue to John is an example.

In	and	and	was
the	the	the	in
beginning	Word	Word	the
was	was	was	beginning
the	with	God.	with
Word,	God,	He	God.

I cannot number the times that I discover a word which shifts my original interpretation to a new perspective by using this method. The same goes for reading the text aloud as I discover voice, emotion, and experience couched deep within the written word.

I suggest selecting the text early in the week – Monday would be great – and writing the text out or copying it onto a small piece of paper to carry around. The text is available for reading over and over and over again. In the familiarity of the text, new insights arise.

Exploring the Text

The exploration of the story is the forensic process by which one discovers the many dimensions of the text. This becomes the CSI (Crime Scene Investigation) approach to scriptural exegesis. It cannot be taken lightly or done in a hit-or-miss fashion. It is more than finding a cute story or maybe the definition of a Greek word.

Often the issue within the text is the cultural milieu, at times strained at being pulled into a different world environment. In the process of this forensic exploration, some questions must be asked of the development of a sermon/proclamation event.

What are the cultural understandings of this text? We take for granted that cultural concepts easily transfer from ancient times to the present. The truth is many of the Gospel stories should create a sense of cultural shock. Jesus talks to a woman when everybody in that culture knows that was against the rules. When the priest and the Levite pass the beaten man on the side of the road, we think they are just cruel, insensitive men. We are not familiar with the implication of action. Those men have a very hard decision to make. What if they touched the man or get blood on their hands and clothes or he dies in their arms? They could not perform their duties in the holy places. Even worse, since he is naked, what if the one beaten is a Samaritan himself!

Knowing the cultural background at times will change the images in the story completely. There are many good resources for finding such information. I find these to be very helpful:

<u>The Dictionary of Biblical Imagery</u>,
    InterVarsity Press
<u>The New Testament: Its Background, Growth, and Content</u>,
    Abingdon Press
<u>The Oxford Companion to the Bible</u>,
    Oxford University Press
<u>Excavating Jesus: Beneath the Stones, Behind the Texts</u>,
    HarperCollins Publishers
<u>Palestine in the Time of Jesus</u>,
    Fortress Press
<u>The Cultural Dictionary of the Bible</u>,
    Liturgical Press

What is the setting of this text? So often we charge forward without understanding where the story fits into the larger picture. Jesus walking on the water in Mark is an interesting story. Jesus had gone up the mountain to pray. The disciples are told to go to the other side, leaving Jesus behind. They are struggling against the wind when suddenly they see Jesus strolling across the water. We often miss the statement "He intended to pass them by" (Mark 6:48

NRSV). Because of their fear, Jesus calls to them to comfort their spirit. He gets into the boat, and suddenly the winds stop. This is a nice story, but it slices between a continuing struggle of the disciples. Prior to the story Jesus had just fed five thousand men. At the end of this water story, when Jesus enters the boat, scripture says, "And they were utterly astounded, for they did not understand about the loaves" (Mark 6:51b - 52aNRSV). So is the story just about Jesus' miraculous walk, or the fearfulness and disbelief of the disciples, or the continued quandary over how a little food fed so many?

This concept is broadened when we ask where this text fits into the big picture. Where does the story fit in the grander scheme? Is Jesus still in Galilee? Is Jesus marching toward Jerusalem? Are the children of Israel still in Egypt or wandering in the wilderness? We need to know the entire landscape of the story, not just the backyard.

There are a number of good commentaries available which approach study in different ways. <u>The New Interpreter's Bible Commentary</u> offers a dual application of scholarly commentary followed by a section on practical application. However, its predecessor <u>The Interpreter's Bible</u> (1952) gives a more scholarly approach to text criticism. <u>The Storyteller's Companion to the Bible</u>, edited by Michael E. Williams, does not cover the entire canon, but I enjoy the inclusion of Jewish midrash stories associated with the Old Testament sections, which again places the story in a different environment. Nothing takes the place of good research. If one knows one's subject well, one is able to present the matter with confidence.

Bridging the Text

After all the investigative work is complete, the next task, critical in the Gospeltelling process, is that of bridging the text. The question must be asked, "How do I transfer an ancient concept into a contemporary understanding?" The response comes from at least three voices.

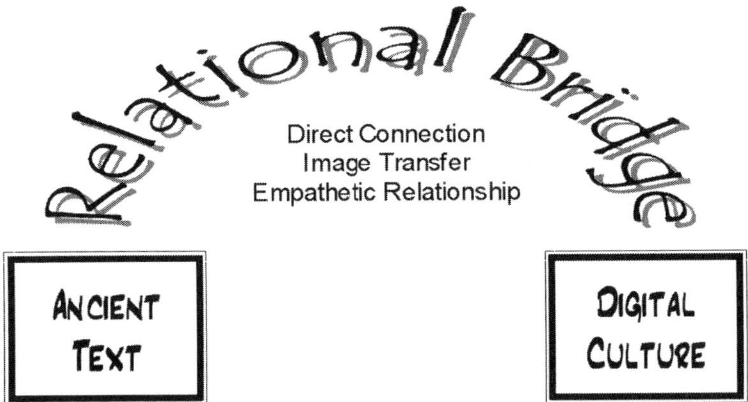

The first voice is that of direct connection. Some texts will still speak plainly and transfer smoothly to the digital culture. When Jesus teaches the people from the mountain in Matthew, he shares examples of what God's people should do and be: "You are the light of the world. A city built on a hill cannot be hid" (Matthew 5:14 NRSV) and "You are like light for the whole world. A city built on top of a hill cannot be hidden" (Matthew 5:14 CEV).

My wife is from North Carolina, and we make the journey from Alabama to North Carolina on a regular basis. That route takes us through the city of Atlanta, Georgia. Going west on Interstate 20, we come to a place where the panorama of the skyline of the city suddenly appears. The view is impressive during the day, but when we reach that spot at night, it is breathtaking. The buildings seem larger-than-life. The gold dome of the Capitol glistens. The tall buildings become towers of light checkerboarded with lights on, lights off areas. The effect is not singular but occurs around numerous large towns and cities. Most persons have had such an experience, so they can make a direct connection of understanding when they hear these words of Jesus – a lighted city on a hill.

Image transfer is another way of crossing the relational bridge. Many stories and parables were set within the context of the agricultural society in which the texts were lived and written. Most post-modern people have a concept of farming, which includes visions of large tractors, combines, and endless fields of corn or wheat. The image of a person walking over dry crusty ground, reaching into a rough bag or bowl, and throwing seeds everywhere is not our first image of a farmer. In fact, those images are associated with struggling third-world countries plagued by drought and disease. The image of the barefoot farmer is linked to the charity organization whose advertising requests money. When the image is not clearly transferable then the image must go through a recasting process. The story of the man who fell among robbers, most commonly called the story of the Good Samaritan, can be a model for image transference.

> Jesus replied, "A man was going down from Jerusalem to Jericho, and fell into the hands of robbers, who stripped him, beat him, and went away, leaving him half dead. Now by chance a priest was going down that road; and when he saw him, he passed by on the other side. So likewise a Levite, when he came to the place and saw him, passed by on the other side. But a Samaritan while traveling came near him; and when he saw him, he was moved with pity. He went to him and bandaged his wounds, having poured oil and wine on them. Then he put him on his own animal, brought him to an inn, and took care of him. The next day he took out two denarii, gave them to the innkeeper, and said, 'Take care of him; and when I come back, I will repay you whatever more you spend.' Which of these three, do you think, was a neighbor to the man who fell into the hands of the robbers?" He said, "The one who showed him mercy." Jesus said to him, "Go and do likewise." (Luke 10:30-37 NRSV)

The story could recast as follows:

A man was going on a business trip and on the way was mugged by a gang who beat him to near death, took all his possessions, even his clothes. Not long after the attack, the pastor of First Church came by and saw the man but did not stop. Soon, a man who was lay leader of his congregation passed that way, but he had things to do and kept going. Finally a Muslim, who also was on a business trip, came to that place and saw the battered and bleeding man. He pulled over and grabbed his first aid kit. He bandaged the man's wounds, put him in his automobile, and took him to the hospital. He sat with the man all night. The next morning he gave the accounting department some money and told the hospital administrator to continue the care. He said he would be back to pay the balance of the bill.

When using image transfer of scripture, it is imperative that the image mirrors the original text. There must be a direct correlation between the image in its original setting and the image in a contemporary setting. If they are not congruent, the image will be confusing since it will relate to something other than the textual implication. I am not saying that we cannot make our own images and parables. It is a wonderful gift to have an imagination which allows us to create new images and concepts, but we must be truthful to the congregation when the image is to reflect the scripture lesson. Later on the side roads and alleys of the Gospeltelling path, personal and borrowed images can be used to complement and clarify the main lesson and its image.

The power of the Gospel and the Word of God did not come to an end when the disciples died. The church canonized a collection of writings as a standard for us. This did not mean that God ceased to use our voices to proclaim the Good News. The personal and prophetic word continues and can be used through the creation of new parables, stories, and metaphors.

We can also bridge the culture through the empathetic relationship. We can paint pretty pictures. We can write beautiful poetry. We can compose enchanting music. But if we do not touch the heart and soul, there is no true connection. Our best efforts are simply "nice" and not meaningful. Emotion is the core of relationship. When we read the bible stories, encased in passion, we connect to them because of our life experiences.

A couple deciding the time is right to have children creates a time of expectation. For some the news of a coming child is almost immediate. For others, it may be a long process and can lead to a time of questioning the inability to bring forth life: "Why can't we have children? Look at Bill and Mary and Sue and Bob. They are expecting. What's wrong?" That emotion brings us into the temple as Hannah[8], a barren wife who lifted up the familiar plea. Her husband Elkanah had two wives. Peninnah had sons and daughters. Hannah had no children. It was evident that she was sad. Brokenhearted, she went to the temple, found a corner, and began praying and weeping, "Lord All-Powerful, I am your servant, but I am miserable! Please let me have a son" (1 Samuel 1:11 CEV). An empathetic relationship is created because most of us have been at a place where we lifted our eyes heavenward and cried to God, "Why?"

Another example of the empathetic relationship is the powerful story of the Jairus whose daughter was near death. Jesus had just crossed the Sea of Galilee and was met by a Jewish leader, who collapsed at his feet. We hear the pain, the brokenness, the despair as he lifts up his request: "My daughter is about to die! Please come, touch her, and make her well."[9]   Parents know the helplessness of struggling with a sick child. I felt so inept in the time when my infant daughters cried from a pain but could not tell me where it hurt. I thought I had crossed the great divide when they were able to speak and say, "It hurts here," but even beyond that point there were pains, physical and emotional, that Daddy could not ease.

The empathetic relationship requires us to respond, "Yes, I know how that feels. I have been down that road. I have experienced being there!" Here is the triunal connection in the Gospeltelling process as we connect with each other and God. I know how I felt in the struggle; you know how you felt; and we all accept the fact that God understands too.

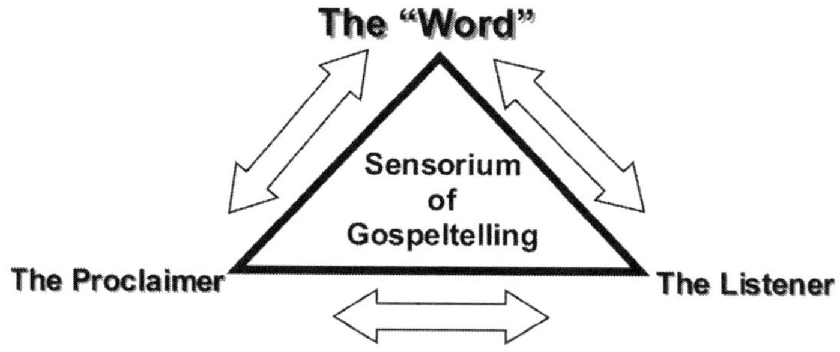

Another method used in the world of media worship is selected video clips. This culture's visual experience is different from all cultures before. The early cave dwellers created "story boards" on stone ceilings and walls relating stories of family, survival, and struggle. Later came writing and the ability to recreate a visual event via written words. We evolved to paintings and photography as a still picture conveyed the story. The movie theater gave us the ability to see action larger-than-life and bigger than any sound experience.   Now with digital technology, we bring those experiences into our homes. The latest trend in storytelling is the ability of the viewer to select the story's end from a variety of options, making it a personal story.

It is within the context of this technology we can find visual bridges. Small clips from familiar movies and programs provide contemporary connections to the text.   With this comes the technology of availability. One can simply go to the Internet site *Google*[10] and search for "video clips for Christian worship." Hundreds of pages of resources appear. Some resources suggest video segments which address the issues of a particular biblical text or theme. Many movies and films can be accessed by simply going to a corner video rental store. I must, however, insert a disclaimer and caution. We must be aware of the copyright laws regarding music and image. We cannot copy video just as we cannot legally make copies of the music sampler meant for preview only. Companies can provide a license giving an organization permission to use selected videos. The Christian Media Association website[11] provides a wide variety of video resources. Lumicon Digital Productions produces in-house media material.[12] Also the site The Text This Week provides both still and media suggestions.[13]

I have a caution about the use of video clips in worship. First, does the clip clearly and plainly express the metaphor needed without having to strain or explain the connection? If there is not a clear-cut connection, then it is like using a story illustration we like when it does not fit the context of the message. We must remember: what we see is what we get - and if the people do not get it, then it is worthless.

Second, and I know this is a bias from my conservative upbringing, is regarding the use of clips from a movie or program. When using a video clip, will you be willing to sanction the viewing of the entire movie or program? Many powerful scenes speak volumes about the issues we face, but will one feel comfortable standing in the presence of the congregation to say "I have watched this movie" and not be ashamed? I know it limits my resources, but I have made the decision not to use a clip if it is from a film or program not suitable for viewing by all those gathered community.

The bridging event calls us to pay attention: pay attention to the place, to the people, to the actions, and to the emotions in the text. What did it mean then? What does it mean now? Where do I find myself in the story? There is a unique power in the Gospel story in that it has the ability to cross that bridge. It has been defined as the "infinite translatability of the Gospels." Face-to-face, heart-to-heart, soul-to-soul, each other in the presence of God – that is Gospeltelling.

Imaging the Text

Aristotle said, "The human soul never thinks without an image, never comprehends without a picture." Hello, Digital Culture! The use of image in worship is commonplace. Once churches hid speakers behind big green plants and drilled holes in everything so that the wires from the microphones were not visible. Today the loudspeakers stand alone, microphones hang from the ceilings, and sometimes a projection screen has taken center stage. PowerPoint has become the stained glass window of the digital culture.

The use of graphics within the entirety of worship is not my focus here but rather the use of media during the proclamation event. Some keep the media involvement simple. The production of a basic PowerPoint[14] slide illustrating the points of a sermons is commonplace. Some use the media screen to make a connection by allowing the listeners a closer view of the proclaimer. Personally, I prefer the image to center on the theme/focus of the message.

I began my multimedia experience with the creation of a PowerPoint slide designed to complement each section/unit of my message. After developing the outline of the message, I went block-by-block seeking images. My problem was not in finding a variety of pictures. One punch of the Internet search button brings up libraries of images, but the pictures themselves are so often from another era. Gustave Dore'[15] illustrated many of the bible stories with grace and integrity in a collection of gray-toned pictures. For the most part, his illustrations accurately portray in context the text in its cultural setting, but others have Jesus marching down the streets with Renaissance maidens and bridled white horses – an incongruent image, at the least. I sought these images building a menagerie of illustration, which seemed to work well if the person running the projector stayed awake and on task.

In later reflections I came to realize that we often experience image overload – too much, too big, too often. We do not give those sitting before us the opportunity to paint their own pictures. I have often returned to the concept of the simple wooden toys, unadorned and elementary in construction. The basis behind the simplicity is that the toy allows children to create, through their imagination, their own concepts of what the toy is to be. The simple wooden car can be an expensive luxury model or a brokendown wreck. The imagination adorns the object according to our own perceptions.

Good verbal skills also add to this experience. In teaching a speech class to college students, I ask, "Describe the sky." Most respond quickly, "It's blue." I then encourage them to paint the sky on the canvas of the listener's imagination. It is a big, blue sky filled with deep white clouds moving rapidly in the direction of the large orange sun sinking over the westward horizon.

Ancient rhetorical teachers would often approach their students and say, "Here is the image – create a speech." In the process of Gospeltelling, many times the concept works backwards. Here is the text, so what is the image?

"What is the image?" is a good question. When we read the text, are we really finding the image of the text, or are we bringing a preconceived image into the text? Years ago I assisted the worship committee of a church in designing banners for the season of Lent. Since these banners were to be used for that and future seasons, I worked from the Gospel lectionary reading of years A, B, and C. I found the first image verbalized was so often not even an image in the text but an image the committee had heard a pastor or preacher allude to in a sermon. We spent much time working through the texts, word-by-word, to carve out authentic images. In the end not only were the banners beautiful, but they also were and would be relevant to the corresponding text.

I suggest simplicity on two levels. First, we should keep the images as simple as possible. I have searched for simple pen-and-ink sketches or even clip art to illustrate the point. Every person paints life with a different brush. One could offer the listeners an outline and let them add the color. I have even used a graphics program to create simple stained glass images. One does not have to be a Rembrandt. One is not required to be a master. We simply offer a basic, elementary image and let the viewers detail the canvas of their imagination.

Epiphany Image

Jesus Walks on the Water

Second, we should keep the images to a minimum. It is not necessary to have an image for every sentence but just enough to illustrate the message. Three or four images may be sufficient. It may be that a single image will capture the essence of what one is trying to say. The purpose is to create a simple, memorable illustration which, if someone asks, "What did the preacher say today?", can be visualized, and one can retell the core of the message. Wilson and Moore affirm this concept:

> When we would develop a successful metaphor at Ginghamsburg Church, people in our congregation could easily recite the crux of a message months later. I heard folks talk about messages from years ago, and it was always tied to the metaphor. Using metaphor to communicate biblical stories allowed us to take what may have been hard or even impossible to understand in today's culture and update it in a way that made sense to everyday people.[16]

There are additional ways to present image other than by a media projector and screen. I began my work with a simple overhead projector illuminating a single slide on the rear wall of the chancel. During the prayer before I began my sermon, a choir member turned on the overhead projector so the people would lift their heads from prayer and see the image. Office supply stores have overhead slide blanks for use in a computer printer. One can find or create an image, print it out, and flash it on the back wall. Another way to present the image is to place it on the front of a worship bulletin or on a banner.

Thomas Troeger says, "God does not conquer by force but by the capturing of the imagination." And how powerfully has that been expressed with the release of Mel Gibson's movie *The Passion*.[17] The original version of the movie was produced in the Aramaic,

Greek, and Hebrew languages. A struggle ensued to add subtitles so persons can follow the story. In an interview Gibson said, "Those who know the story will not need to understand the words." In a masterful way he accomplished that storyline.

The digital culture is nothing more than a remix of the oral culture. Both rely on a person's ability to interpret image. A single image can tell the entire story.

Proclaiming the Text

Once the forensic work is done, the next step is to put the work in a form for oral presentation. As so many of the other homileticians have noted, there is no "right" and "only" way of proclamation. It is a personal process and must be congruent with a person's personality. One may do one's best work when lifting the proclamation from a complete manuscript, standing behind the pulpit, vested to the highest order. One may work better from memory while standing on the front of a stage or chancel exposed to everyone and trusting in God to keep one's mind on track. One may stand somewhere in between, and that is all right. One might enjoy the scholarly challenge of a deep, expository sermon. One might like the freedom of proclaiming from an outline with points one, two, and three. One may enjoy losing one's self in a narrative as one becomes a voice for others. And all this is fine, too. The bottom line is that one feels good about how one proclaims the Gospel. Dr. Robert Mulholland once said, "If they see the incarnation of Scripture (in you), then they will listen to your proclamation of scripture."

Personally, I stand in the center of the chancel, holding a bible where my outline is inserted, and offer the message in primarily an epideictic formula – introduction, body, and conclusion. After setting the stage for the main focus, I do not go from point one to two to three but rather move with verbal threads of "then" and "next" and "so." Each step of the journey should be an awakening moment. I have admired Garrison Keillor's storytelling for years. He has a wonderful way of telling a story which branches and divides over and over during the journey but eventually returns home for the final "oh." My sermon/proclamation style is similar. As I carry the congregation on a journey, I often turn down a side alley to explore or experience something which will be valuable when we get back on the main road.

I need to share some directional thoughts general in nature but specific to the proclamation moment. The first of these thoughts concerns the scripture itself. If we are going to read the text, then we should read it well. We should know the text well enough to add voice and color, to raise the voice and shadow the voice as the text requires. If we memorize the text of the day, then we must know the story well enough to make the story become our own story. We should not worry if the story is exactly as printed in the chosen translation. Worrying about absolute textual accuracy can lead to frustration and unneeded anxiety. We should live with the text and make it our own while staying true and allowing the text to flow. We should "tell" the story.

The second point has to do with assumptions. Power comes from familiarity, and we should not assume people know the story. Recently, I was watching a female preacher running up and down the stage as she proclaimed her thoughts on a Godly marriage. At one point she referred to a story in the Old Testament with the remark, "I am not going to tell you the whole story. You already know it." Well, that is a big assumption. I enjoy using biblical illustrations. There is a power in the connectedness of scripture when we can stand proclaiming the word from the New Covenant and support our thoughts with illustrations from the Old Covenant. But when we do, we must be sure to tell the whole story.

When we as proclaimer/preachers develop a message, we let that message lead the people on a journey – not push them down the road. We give the listeners the ability to walk beside us and even have their own personal experiences on the way. Michael Williams says, "What the listener brings to the story is just as important as what the storyteller brings."[18] We should lead people through the story, not preach at them. When we fall into the pit of "preaching at" the people, we are in danger of proclaiming our personal words over the Word of God. We should remember the prophet's cry, "Thus says the Lord."

We should become physically involved with the message. Storyteller Jay O'Callahan says that storytelling (for me Gospeltelling) is a theater of the face. Emotion breeds emotion. Passion fuels passion. Storytelling is not cranial but experiential. There is a need for caution. When tellers share the story with emotion, they should be sure the actions on faces, voices, and gestures are congruent with what is said. Without emotion and passion, the message is just another story. The opportunity to proclaim the Word of God is too important to treat simply as fairytale or bedside story. It must become Good News – Gospel.

Finally, Leonard Sweet says, "God did not send us a statement. God sent us a story."[19] The Gospel story is not passed down page-by-page but heart-to-heart. And Gospeltelling is the proclamation moment couched in a multisensory event. The place, the smells, the sounds, the visuals, the proclamation, all blend into a single event. It is what creates the atmosphere for which that triunal connection happens: the place where the proclaimer, listener, and God find themselves standing face-to-face and heart-to-heart.

Chapter 4 Endnotes

1. Steven Spielberg, dir., *Hook*, Columbia/Tristar, 1991.
2. Wilson and Moore, Digital Storytellers, 163.
3. Percentages calculated by D. Jonathan Watts.
4. Slaughter, Out on the Edge, 123.
5. Kimball, Emerging Worship, 104.
6. The National Bible Society, http://www.nationalbible.com/dbc/info/versioncev.php3.
7. Katherine Veach, "Early Bible Translations Losing Popularity," Birmingham News, section C10, Saturday, August 28, 2004.
8. The story of Hannah is found in 1 Samuel chapter 1.
9. The story of the found in Mark 5:21-24, 35-43.
10. Google, www.google.com.
11. Christian Media Association, http://www.churchvideoassociation.com/.
12. Lumicon Digital Productions, http://www.lumicon.org/index.asp.
13. The Text This Week, http://www.textweek.com/.
14. Microsoft PowerPoint software, Microsoft Corporation.
15. Gustave Dore', http://myweb.lmu.edu/fjust/Dore.htm.
16. Wilson and Moore, 34.
17. Mel Gibson, dir., *The Passion*, Icon Productions, 2004.
18. Michael Williams, St*orytelling: A Journey into New Worlds* video, 1998.
19. Sweet, Quantum Spirituality, 81.

CHAPTER 5
THE FORENSIC RECONSTRUCTION OF A GOOD STORY
An Exploration of Luke 15:11-32

Chapter 3 presented a variety of preaching/proclamation styles. The style a person uses or develops is indeed personal. Some may be comfortable with the free-flowing nature of the narrative style while others prefer the framework of the expository pattern moving from point to point. Chapter 4 offered a methodology for the presentation of the word/sermon in a multimedia context. This chapter will provide a model for the forensic exploration of the text, which prepares for the development of the proclamation event.

This chapter will move through four steps of the forensic reconstruction of the story. "Forensic" means the careful and methodical examination of a text. We so often hear that word used for criminal investigations as the forensic process produces evidence for a case. For the preaching/proclamation event, we need to be aware of the text. We must look below the surface, examine the context, emotion, and intent of the text. Then there must be a reconstruction of the story tuned for the ear and eye of a digital culture.

The process of forensic reconstruction will be reading the text, examining the text, forensically investigating of the text, and, finally, sharing the text.

Reading The Text

To put into praxis the methodology of Gospeltelling, I will use the text of Luke 15:11-32 as a model. This particular text is the lectionary reading for Year C, the fourth Sunday in Lent. It is the longest single parable Jesus told. I will present the text in two versions, the New Revised Standard Version (a text often used for critical exegesis) and the Contemporary English Version (a version designed for the ear).

Luke 15:11-32 NRSV

[11]Then Jesus said, 'There was a man who had two sons. [12]The younger of them said to his father, "Father, give me the share of the property that will belong to me." So he divided his property between them. [13]A few days later the younger son gathered all he had and traveled to a distant country, and there he squandered his property in dissolute living. [14]When he had spent everything, a severe famine took place throughout that country, and he began to be in need. [15]So he went and hired himself out to one of the citizens of that country, who sent him to his fields to feed the pigs. [16]He would gladly have filled himself with the pods that the pigs were eating; and no one gave him anything. [17]But when he came to himself he said, "How many of my father's hired hands have bread enough and to spare, but here I am dying of hunger! [18]I will get up and go to my father, and I will say to him, 'Father, I have sinned against heaven and before you; [19]I am no longer worthy to be called your son; treat me like one of your hired hands.'" [20]So he set off and went to his father. But while he was still far off, his father saw him and was filled with compassion; he ran and put his arms around him and kissed him. [21]Then the son said to him, "Father, I have sinned against heaven and before you; I am no longer worthy to be called your son." [22]But the father said to his slaves, "Quickly, bring out a robe—the best one—and put it on him; put a ring on his finger and sandals on his feet. [23]And get the fatted calf and kill it, and let us eat and celebrate; [24]for this son of mine was dead and is alive again; he was lost and is found!" And they began to celebrate.

[25]'Now his elder son was in the field; and when he came and approached the house, he heard music and dancing. [26]He called one of the slaves and asked what was going on. [27]He replied, "Your brother has come, and your father has killed the fatted calf, because he has got him back safe and sound." [28]Then he became angry and refused to go in. His father came out and began to plead with him. [29]But he answered his father, "Listen! For all these years I have been working like a slave for you, and I have never disobeyed your command; yet you have never given me even a young goat

so that I might celebrate with my friends. [30]But when this son of yours came back, who has devoured your property with prostitutes, you killed the fatted calf for him!" [31]Then the father said to him, "Son, you are always with me, and all that is mine is yours. [32]But we had to celebrate and rejoice, because this brother of yours was dead and has come to life; he was lost and has been found."'

Luke 15:11-32 CEV

[11]Jesus also told them another story:

Once a man had two sons. [12]The younger son said to his father, "Give me my share of the property." So the father divided his property between his two sons.

[13]Not long after that, the younger son packed up everything he owned and left for a foreign country, where he wasted all his money in wild living. [14]He had spent everything, when a bad famine spread through that whole land. Soon he had nothing to eat.

[15]He went to work for a man in that country, and the man sent him out to take care of his pigs. [16]He would have been glad to eat what the pigs were eating, but no one gave him a thing.

[17]Finally, he came to his senses and said, "My father's workers have plenty to eat, and here I am, starving to death! [18]I will go to my father and say to him, 'Father, I have sinned against God in heaven and against you. [19]I am no longer good enough to be called your son. Treat me like one of your workers.'"

[20]The younger son got up and started back to his father. But when he was still along way off, his father saw him and felt sorry for him. He ran to his son and hugged and kissed him.

[21]The son said, "Father, I have sinned against God in heaven and against you. I am no longer good enough to be called your son."

[22]But his father said to the servants, "Hurry and bring the best clothes and put them on him. Give him a ring for his finger and sandals for his feet. [23]Get the best calf and prepare it, so we can eat and celebrate. [24]This son of mine was dead,

but has now come back to life. He was lost and has now been found." And they began to celebrate.

[25]The older son had been out in the field. But when he came near the house, he heard the music and dancing. [26]So he called one of the servants over and asked, "What's going on here?"

[27]The servant answered, "Your brother has come home safe and sound, and your father ordered us to kill the best calf." [28]The older brother got so angry that he would not even go into the house.

His father came out and begged him to go in. [29]But he said to his father, "For years I have worked for you like a slave and have always obeyed you. But you have never even given me a little goat, so that I could give a dinner for my friends. [30]This other son of yours wasted your money on prostitutes. And now that he has come home, you ordered the best calf to be killed for a feast."

[31]His father replied, "My son, you are always with me, and everything I have is yours. [32]But we should be glad and celebrate! Your brother was dead, but he is now alive. He was lost and has now been found."

Examining the Text

The next step in the process is to examine the text. When reading the text, we become aware of the tension experienced in each setting. We can visually see a difference in the way the two versions punctuate the story. In the NRSV the story is comprised of only two paragraphs. The first paragraph is the story of the younger son, and the second paragraph is the story of the older son. Visually, the NRSV seems to run everything together. The CEV appears to take its time, inserting paragraph indentions as a way of catching our breath or slowing the pace of the story.

The parable can be divided into event blocks: the crisis of the son's asking for the inheritance; the arrogance and collapse of the younger son; the humility and decision to return home; the acceptance of his homecoming; and the anger and hostility of the older son. These emotions are best felt when released into the air, in an oral production of the story later.

I have found it helpful to copy and print the text on my

computer. Through the wizardry of computer technology, I break the text into vocal or transitional segments. I then use the text-coloring feature of most word processing programs and color the reading into voices and movement. If there are several voices, then I select a color for each voice, to visually see the shift. We hear the voice of the narrator (the voice of Jesus), the father, the younger son, the older son, and, briefly, the voice of a servant. The highlighting or coloring of the text assists in the oral production as we visually experience the changing voices within the story.

I also plot the story. Creating a story timeline assists in visualizing the progression of the parable from beginning to end. Visually, this particular parable is better to plot vertically rather than horizontally. I place the father as the constant in the center of the timeline. On each side of the father is a son, each having his own story. At the crisis points we see the father standing as the central figure.

Here is my plotting of the story:

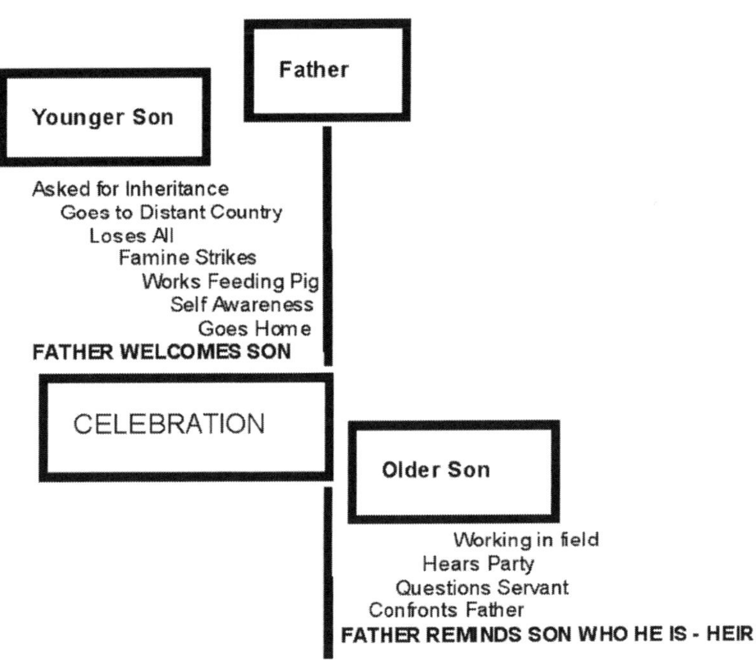

I try to imagine how Jesus would have told the story. Did he use a strong voice or a soft, captivating tone? Was Jesus talking to a few or calling out to the masses? Was he teaching his disciples or issuing warnings to those who were constantly putting him to the test? To answer those questions, we must step back from the text to get a larger picture of the setting of the text.

When we seek to find the setting and context of the text, we look for those transitory words, such as <u>then</u>, <u>next</u>, and <u>later</u>. The previous chapter begins "On one occasion." Jesus had been invited to the house of a leader of the Pharisees to eat a meal on the sabbath. We so often find our teeth on edge any time we hear the words "Jesus" and "Pharisee" in the same sentence. Theologically they were on the same page. Unlike the Sadducees, who were the old Torah people who did not believe in an afterlife, Pharisees believed not only in an afterlife but also that the afterlife carried with it the element of judgment – reward or punishment for eternity. The presence of Pharisees occurred on many occasions because they were interested in one who shared a theological foundation, but we also we experience over and over again the expression found in Luke 14:1b: "...they were watching him closely." Jesus did not hesitate to challenge and/or chastise them when the opportunity arose.

Seeing a man suffering from dropsy, a swelling from excessive accumulation of serous fluid in tissue now called edema, Jesus makes the first challenge around the table by asking the lawyers and Pharisees about the legality of healing on the sabbath. This is followed by Jesus's noticing how people chose their seats at the gathering. In response to their actions, Jesus tells them a parable about how persons should choose the lower seat and be invited up to the head table with honor rather than rush to the head table and be embarrassed when asked to move. Immediately, he tells another parable about one who gave a great dinner and invited many who responded with excuses for not being able to attend.

In Luke 14:25: we experience a transition. "Now large crowds were traveling with him." Suddenly we question the route. Where were they going? That answer comes further back in Luke 9:51: "When the days drew near for him to be taken up, he set his face toward Jerusalem." Passing through a village in Samaria, he began his journey to Jerusalem for the last time (or the first time since he was in the Temple as a boy, according to Luke). Jesus teaches the crowd as they travel: "Whoever does not carry the cross and follow me cannot be my disciple" (Luke 14:27 NRSV) and "Salt is good;

but if salt has lost its taste, how can its saltiness be restored?" (Luke 14:34 NRSV).

Chapter 15 begins "Now all the tax collectors and sinners were coming near to listen to him" (Luke 15:1 NRSV). If we begin with Chapter 15:1, we get the feeling that Jesus was at someone's home dining with tax collectors and sinners, but by reviewing the setting of the text, we see that Jesus may be continuing on his journey and where people appear to gravitate towards the traveling seminary. Is this parable being told "on the road" or is it a dinner conversation? We could argue for the dinner setting since the issue of Jesus welcoming sinners and eating with them is raised by the Pharisees and scribes. We do not get the complete setting until Luke 17:11. There we see Jesus "on the way to Jerusalem" as he travels through the regions between Samaria and Galilee, so this parable seems to be told on the road somewhere between Galilee and Jerusalem.

As the "undesirables" gathered around Jesus, the "holy ones" began to grumble. Maybe we have had that feeling. We and our friends are somewhere when another group of people begins to invade our space. Maybe they are not like us and our friends. Maybe they come from the proverbial "other side of the tracks." Maybe they have different social values. Maybe we just do not like them. Whatever it is, we begin to feel uncomfortable and really wish they would go away. If we have had this experience, and most of us have, then here is one of the empathetic connections to the story. Not that we want to be on the side of the Pharisees and scribes, just that we may be able to relate to how they were feeling.

In the introduction of the preceding parables, Jesus puts those complainers in unwanted positions. First, he illustrates a parable which asks them to take the role of a shepherd. That is not a flattering image. Shepherds at this point in history did not have the grandest reputations, and to place those who thought highly of themselves in this position was, at the least, degrading. In the following parable he skirts the direct implication, but the feeling is still there when Jesus begins, "Or what woman ... ." He does not use the phrase "which one of you," but the implication is that they are to put themselves in the position of the woman who has lost the coin. This is something these men would not easily accept, so Jesus has them on edge as he continues telling the parables.

Immediately after the telling of the textual parable, Jesus continues to teach. He tells about a dishonest manager (Luke 16:1-

13), following with some short sayings. He tells the parable of the rich man and Lazarus, painting a picture of the afterlife. It is after that story, mentioned earlier (Luke 17:11), that we see Jesus continuing down the road toward Jerusalem.

Now that we have an understanding of where this text fits into the larger picture, it is time to critically examine the text itself.

The Forensic Investigation of the Text

It has been repeated so many times: "Study to show yourself approved." The study needed to prepare for and present the Word requires devotion. For most of us, if we attempted to create a sermon/homily with nothing in front of us but the text, it would indeed be a shallow presentation. Just as God has called some to be teachers, proclaimers, preachers of the Word, God has also called those who have the gift of inquisitiveness. These persons spend a lifetime digging up history and struggling with language so the Word can become clearer. We should use the wisdom of those called to that task.

The third parable in the trilogy of the lost is about a trio of persons – a father, a younger son, and an older son. The stage regarding the issues of shame and honor needs to be set immediately for the western culture. It is not that unusual to read in the paper or hear of the abusiveness of eastern family members against their own children or siblings. If a daughter steps outside the father's wishes and meets with a person deemed undesirable, she may be beaten or even mutilated. Sometimes the penalty is so harsh it results in the death of the daughter. The reason for such drastic conduct is the action's reflection on the honor of the family. This continues to be played out today in the conflict between Israel and Palestine. As soon as someone on one side gets injured or killed, the other side responds with taking equal or greater action. The cycle created never stops: You hurt me and I hurt you and you hurt someone else and I retaliate. The bottom line to this cycle perpetuates the idea of "honor above all."

What is at issue here is not so much the loss of money or waste of family wealth. The core issue is that of family honor and how Jesus portraits a shift in the societal paradigm.

Then Jesus said, 'There was a man who had two sons. The

younger of them said to his father, "Father, give me the share of the property that will belong to me." So he divided his property between them. (Luke 15:11-12 NRSV)

This is a most shocking introduction to a parable. One can talk about heaven and houses and livestock. We never talk about the inheritance. Barry Kiger, with the Jerusalem Center for Biblical Studies, says this is an absolutely unbelievable story because so many cultural boundaries are being crossed.[1]

When we hear the words "younger son" and listen to his words, we create an image of a youthful young man. Joachim Jeremias says that since the son appears to be unmarried, he would probably be eighteen to twenty years of age.[2] He may be tired of working with and for an older brother. Maybe as he moves from adolescence to manhood, he wants his independence, although the attitude portrayed does indeed have a less-than-mature feel. Here again, it is a parable, and as listeners we are at liberty to paint the picture within our own images and imagination.

When it comes to the inheritance, the law is specific. Deuteronomy 21 establishes the dictates of inheritance: Where there are two sons, the elder receives two-thirds of the total inheritance and the younger receives one-third. The inheritance is composed of both fixed and liquid assets. Barns, fields, and houses are fixed; livestock, jewels, and money are liquid. When the inheritance is divided, one party could receive a share from the liquid portion, which seems to be the intended case in this parable.

It was possible for the inheritance to be divided before the death of a father. Maybe a father sees promise in a younger son and gives him a portion of the inheritance to begin his own business or farm. The dividing of the inheritance is not the key issue here. Charles Page notes, "It was legal for a son to receive his inheritance early, but for him to ask for it would have been perceived as wishing the father were dead."[3] When the younger son asks the question lightning would have struck in the souls of the listeners. If one needs money, one just asks for money, but asking for the inheritance brings with it a crushing weight. Here, says Jeremias, the younger son "demands not only the right of possession but the right of disposal."[4]

Again here is an empathetic connection. Most of us have had parental conflict. I remember, as a teenager, the tension between my father and me when I was told "no" to the things I wanted so badly to do or to have. Yes, I became really angry from time to time, but I never remember getting so angry that I was willing to declare, "Dad, I wish you were dead!" As a parent, I have become very angry at my children but never once wished they would just disappear. Shame. Honor. Crisis.

To the amazement of the Pharisees and scribes, they hear the father in the parable respond by dividing the inheritance. This is the flip side of the coin. Kiger says the action is called *kezazah,* or the breaking of the pot, and this action represents the disappearance of a person.[5]   In the end, from a cultural view, the father is dead in the eyes of the son and the son has never existed in the eyes of the father.

"So he divided his property between them." This is a parable, not a true story. In a parable we can bend the rules and suspend the norms. If it were a true story, we would wonder why the older brother did not appear earlier in the story to try to stop this tragedy between a father and son. Surely, he realized that the property was being divided.

A few days later the younger son gathered all he had and traveled to a distant country, and there he squandered his property in dissolute living. (Luke 15:13 NRSV)

The insulant son cashes in the liquid assets, packs his bags, and gets out of town. Many define that "distant country" as Gentile territory, foreshadowing the event of his forced vocation. The Interpreter's Bible commentary says, "Jesus' hearers would think of such lands as Italy, North Africa, Egypt, or even Babylonia."[6]   We can only speculate on the geographical setting of the parable. Jesus does not tell us the specific town or territory of origin. The distant place puts the younger son in a community where he would be without honor or status.

I personally vision the "squandering" as not simply one long wild party but rather an attempt for this younger son to buy his honor in another town. Thomas Boomershine writes, "There is no necessary implication in the phrase usually translated as 'loose living' that he spend the money immorally. The only exegetical basis for this reading is the older brother's later statement that he wasted the inheritance with prostitutes."[7]   Maybe he thought he would have enough to purchase a place of prominence and have some resources left over for future investment. It may have been a shock to realize that suddenly all was gone and he had absolutely nothing to show for it. Here we experience a connection as we cross the Relational Bridge. To use a colloquial term, when the a person is "broke" it carries the same feeling today as it did two thousand years ago.

When he had spent everything, a severe famine took place throughout that country, and he began to be in need. So he went and hired himself out to one of the citizens of that country, who sent him to his fields to feed the pigs. He would gladly have filled himself with the pods that the pigs were eating; and no one gave him anything. (Luke 15: 14-16 NRSV)

Just when he thinks things could not get any worse, they get worse. He has spent everything, and he can blame no one but himself. Now something out of his control affects his life as a severe famine takes its hold on the land. He is starving and needy. Where can he turn? I am sure this was the feeling of those riding the economical high before the crash of the stock market. They felt secure. They felt in control. They never saw the tragedy coming. Suddenly retirement funds disappeared. College savings vanished. "What do I do now?" came bursting forth from so many souls. He has lost everything. A direct link between the ancient story and the digital culture again is found. And when all was gone – all was gone.

Broke and broken, he desperately seeks a way to survive. Maybe he sits at the town gate with a sign around his neck: "Will work for food." In desperation he hires himself out to a citizen of the distant land. In a society of honor, he has hit bottom. A hired hand does not have the rights of a slave. He is at the complete mercy of the master. Charles H. Tabert notes: "The polite way a Mid-Easterner gets rid of unwanted hangers-on is by assigning them a task he knows they will refuse."[8] It may have surprised the citizen that the wayward Jewish man would accept such employment.

I pastored a church in an area which relied heavily on the income produced by the poultry industry. Because of the nature of the work, few local laborers wanted to be employed at the plants. As a result, an inpouring of Hispanic workers took the positions. I often heard the challenge that the immigrants were stealing American jobs, but an equally quick response came "They are doing jobs no one else will do." The emotional impact here is that the son not only was offered a job which no one wanted to do but, because of his own actions, he was also forced to accept the employment.

The employment was to tend the pigs. In his book <u>Hear Then the Parable</u>, Bernard Scott cites a talmudic teaching instructing the Jewish community that say, "None may rear swine anywhere."[9] He follows that by quoting a curse: "Cursed be the man who would breed swine."[10] The son has now hit bottom – no money, no friends, and no self-respect.

We so often see in our imagination the son in the pen with cute little pink pigs. Nothing could be further from the truth. Pigs are not cute pink creatures but rather dirty and disgusting. The continual grunting is tiring and the smell of the pigs and what they leave behind will quickly turn the most iron stomachs weak. By the time this parable is told we experience the domestication of pigs, illustrated in the miracle of the possessed man in the country side of the Gerasenes. Jesus is confronted by the spirits and he casts them into a herd of swine.[11] After the two thousand swine run into the sea, the owners of the swine tell Jesus to leave the country. They could not afford the loss of an agricultural industry. In the ancient world pigs would roam the streets with the wild dogs scavenging for food. H .N. Wendt says the pigs "served as the community's garbage disposal units." [12] Pigs were herded similar to the fashion of sheep. There were no fences and pens; the son's job was to chase after the pigs keeping them in some sense of restraint.

The depth of despair comes in the statement "He would gladly have filled himself with the pods that the pigs were eating." Life can get so critical that a person is willing to do anything to survive. I have often told people not to judge too quickly those caught in situations such as embezzling money, never to say, "I'd never do that!" We do not know what we would do if we become desperate enough.

He was willing to eat the food the pigs were eating, and no one gave him anything. I have often wondered if, in the struggle to herd the wayward pigs, he would hold out his hand to those passing, by only to have his plea for help rejected. It is amazing that even here he hung on to a small shred of dignity. It did not say he ate the pig food, only that he thought about it.

But when he came to himself he said, "How many of my father's hired hands have bread enough and to spare, but here I am dying of hunger! I will get up and go to my father, and I will say to him, 'Father, I have sinned against heaven and before you; I am no longer worthy to be called your son; treat me like one of your hired hands.'" (Luke 15:17-19)

"But when he came to himself." The light of the soul which illuminates hope switches on. But what threw the switch? It could have been the son remembered an ancient Israelite saying: "When an Israelite stoops so low as eat carob beans, then he will return home." What are carob beans? Food for the livestock – the pigs. His awareness returned to him when he almost ate the food but did not. He realizes that even in his condition, he is still a child of Abraham.

Reaching the point of starvation, the son remembers his home-cooked meals, always enough to go around – and some to spare. A Talmudic proverb says, "When a son [who has left home] has to walk barefooted [because of poverty], he remembers how well he had been treated in his father's home."[13]

"When he came to himself" carries more weight than simply an idea or the changing of the mind. <u>The Dictionary of Biblical Imagery</u> says, that "repentance involves the whole person - mind, heart, and will – and it is possible that he is returning to his father with the goal of repaying his debt through work."[14] Again we are reminded that this is a parable. We have the right to paint this story with our own colors and hues without infringing on the image another has created. The image of those thoughts stirs in the son enough courage to dare to go home. So he begins rehearsing a confrontational speech in the hope that his father will listen.

I remember as a child, and even as an adult, rehearsing my defense. I would play the scene over in my mind. I would imagine how the conversation would start and then move to the issue at hand. I could imagine making my plea and it being successful: "Father, I have sinned against heaven and before you; I am no longer worthy to be called your son; treat me like one of your hired hands." The son had sinned against heaven when he wished his father dead and against his father when he wasted the inheritance. With these confessions implanted in his very soul, he is willing to take a position lower than a slave. At least, he would have a place to live and enough food to eat.

I have heard this text read on many occasions, and more often than not this statement is rushed. This is a pivotal statement. The younger son has just had an epiphany. He is gathering his courage and planning the point of contact. He must convince his father to allow him to return to the farm, the same father he declared dead and whose life's wealth he squandered. Besides, if he is allowed to return home, he will have to work under the supervision of his older brother.

So he set off and went to his father. (Luke 15:20a NRSV)

There is no other way. He has to go home. He gathers his speech, puts it in his ragged pocket, and sets out on his journey. They say the first step is always the hardest. We never hear him return to the "citizen" and tell him that he will have to find another swine herder. He may have paused just a moment to kiss a pig and say, "Thanks for bringing me to my senses." With a humble boldness, he travels home.

But while he was still far off, his father saw him and was filled with compassion; he ran and put his arms around him and kissed him. (Luke 15:20b NRSV)

So often we hear this verse and imagine a father who has been sitting on the front porch mournfully wishing for the son to return. The way I read the text, that posture is not in the picture. We must remember the father has "broken the pot" and, to the best of his ability, has written his son out of the family history. However, that is not to say that once in a while he does not lift an eye toward the "far country," hoping to one day see a son return, cloaked in his success. When he lifts his eyes to see his son coming home, it is not a pretty sight. His son is dirty and gaunt, laboring with each step. I hear the voice of a passionate father, "Oh, son!" Recognizing the trauma, the father breaks into a run.

Several issues surface with the running of the father. The first has to do with dignity. A man of honor never runs. Sirach 19:30 instructs "A man's manner of walking tells you what he is." The father sacrifices his dignity to meet his son on the homeward road.

Another issue raised by Charles Page, Dean of the Jerusalem

Center for Biblical Studies, is the response of the community. He explains how in the shame/honor cultic system, when one harms the family, one harms the entire community: "Contemporary Arabs have interpreted the reason why the father runs to meet his son in this manner as meaning that the son will be protected by the father from the other men of the village, who would, under law, stone the son to death."[15]   The basis for this action is found in Deuteronomy 21:18-21 NRSV:

> If someone has a stubborn and rebellious son who will not obey his father and mother, who does not heed them when they discipline him, then his father and his mother shall take hold of him and bring him out to the elders of his town at the gate of that place. They shall say to the elders of his town, 'This son of ours is stubborn and rebellious. He will not obey us. He is a glutton and a drunkard.' Then all the men of the town shall stone him to death. So you shall purge the evil from your midst; and all Israel will hear, and be afraid.

He has brought dishonor to the family and to the community, and a penalty must be paid. In fear of this happening, the father runs and embraces the son. With the embrace comes the shrouding of the son in the father's robe. He is being protected by the one he had dishonored. The one who now is holding him close and kissing him has become his safeguard. Charles H. Tabert says that the father's embrace would have kept the weak and weary son from falling to his knees.[16] It is a scene of reconciliation. The estranged son has come home. The father has opened his arms and has protected him from harm.

The empathetic connection here is at the point of reconciliation. Most of us have had disagreements with friends or family, maybe even to a point of not speaking. A crack in a relationship quickly becomes a great chasm. There is pain in estrangement. There is agony in separation. There is the struggle of what to do, what to say, what to think. Occasionally something comes crashing in and the two come face-to-face. Letting down their guard, they experience reconciliation and, more often than not, find within it the question of "why did this happen?"

Bernard Scott relays a story from the rabbinical tradition: "A king had a son who had gone astray from his father a journey of a hundred days; his friends said to him, 'Return home to your father,' he said, 'I cannot.' Then his father sent to say, 'Return as far as you can, and I will come to you the rest of the way.' So God says, 'Return to me, and I will return to you.'"[17]

I have heard story after story of the tough-love of parents for wayward children. Not long ago I talked with a parent who had struggled with a daughter on drugs. He and his wife did everything they knew to do to help the daughter get the demon off her back, but the daughter would never follow through with her side of the commitment. Eventually, the parents, on the daughter's eighteenth birthday, packed up her room and placed the items on the front porch with a note: "Come back when you get it all together."

The daughter disappeared for several years, living out the results of addiction. But one day she woke from the horrors and began to correct her path. She called her parents and came home. The reconciliation was a powerful moment. The daughter then went to college and graduate school, eventually becoming an attorney who works with addicted children.

The return of the son two thousand years ago and the return of the child two weeks ago have the same emotional impact. The father runs to the son, and in that intimate moment, he embraces him and kisses him. The kiss is significant. Talbert says, "A kiss on the cheek was a sign of reconciliation and forgiveness."[18] The shattered fabric of the family is mended.

Then the son said to him, "Father, I have sinned against heaven and before you; I am no longer worthy to be called your son." But the father said to his slaves, "Quickly, bring out a robe— the best one—and put it on him; put a ring on his finger and sandals on his feet. And get the fatted calf and kill it, and let us eat and celebrate; for this son of mine was dead and is alive again; he was lost and is found!" (Luke 15: 21-24a NRSV)

Apparently, while still in the embrace, the son tries to state his case but gets through only the first half, never reaching the part of becoming a hired hand. It appears the father is not alone in the embracing moment since, as he stops his son's declaration, he addresses the servants who are there with them. The normal signs of hospitality would be a hug and a kiss, oil for his head, and water to wash his feet. Instead, the father commands the servant to fetch three articles to bring about the re-entry into the family.

The New Interpreter's Bible commentary defines the best robe as either the best robe of the father or the best robe which belonged to the son before his departure.[19]   Dr. Evelyn Laycock, who was a Professor of Religion at Hiwassee College for thirty-five years, says one interpretation of the best robe could be the tallit or prayer shawl which gained its value by being passed down generation to generation. Her statement is backed up by the thoughts of Charles Page: "We might imagine that the father gave his son a tallit, the prayer shawl that symbolizes the keeping of the covenant. By giving his son his own tallit, or prayer shawl, the father symbolically welcomes his son back to the covenant people, the people of God."[20]

If this is to be considered a legitimate interpretation, there would be a crisis involved in this action. By first century standards, the tallit is now property of his older son, but in defense of this statement, the text does not say "give" the son the robe but simply "put" the robe on him. This could be received as a symbolic gesture, bringing him back under the umbrella of God's grace.

If the robe is not the tallit, then it is a very special robe. Jeremias tells about the ceremonial robe of that culture: "The ceremonial robe, . . . in the East is a mark of high distinction. . . . when the king wishes to honour a deserving official, he presents him a costly robe."[21]

Along with the robe, the son is given a signet ring, which returns his family authority. He is given shoes, which make him more than a slave. Finally, the father instructs the servant to kill the fatted calf and have a party. The son has been restored with the closing statement of the scene: "for this son of mine was dead and is alive again; he was lost and is found."

Terrence W. Tilly gives this analogy:

A clear modern parallel is to imagine a teenager, driving the family car home about three in the morning after an evening of riotous partying, being greeted by an anxious parent who sweeps the prodigal up in his arms, whirls him around and busts out, 'Thank God you're home! Let's have a party to celebrate!' The action of the father in Jesus' story is just as bewildering.[22]

And they began to celebrate. (Luke 15:24b NRSV)

Evelyn Laycock, in her lectures at Hewett United Methodist Church, listed the expectations of the celebrations. If a person decided to have a gathering of two to four people, one would cook a chicken. A gathering of five to eight guests required a duck. If there were nine to fifteen people, a kid or small goat was prepared. A lamb was slaughtered for a gathering of sixteen to thirty-five. And for the big party of thirty-six or more, the fatted calf was killed.[23] According to the <u>Dictionary of Biblical Imagery</u>, the fatted calf was a grain-fed calf kept in a stall so it would remain untainted by unwanted exposure. It was a symbol of hospitality and celebration. A feast built around the fatted calf could include as many as two hundred people.[24] When the father called for the fatted calf to be slaughtered, he was preparing for a big celebration.

Tony Campolo says Jesus was destined to be either a Jew or an Italian because they were the two nationalities that really knew how to party – and Jesus loved to party. The call from the parable seems exciting – "And they began to celebrate!" The feast was not a simple gathering from six o'clock until ten o'clock one evening but a celebration lasting for days. The people gathered for the meal, and after they had eaten their fill, they began to sing and dance.

This would have been such a great place to end the parable. The son has come home. The father has reinstated his son to a rightful position. The community has been called together to celebrate the reconciliation. But the story is not over.

Now his elder son was in the field; and when he came and approached the house, he heard music and dancing. He called one of the slaves and asked what was going on. He replied, "Your brother has come, and your father has killed the fatted calf, because he has got him back safe and sound." Then he became angry and refused to go in. (Luke 15:25-28 NRSV)

The older brother is taking care of business. The impression is that the homestead is large enough for the elder son to be working and not notice the preparations for the celebration nor the gathering crowd. In the parable it seems as if the father calls for the celebration to take place within a matter of minutes. But it takes time. The calf has to be slaughtered and prepared. The invitation has to go out to the community. The people in the community, in a state of surprise, must have time to clean up and dress for the event. It would have been very time-consuming, but again we are reminded that this is a parable so real time has been suspended.

As the older son wanders home he is shocked by what he hears – the music and the dancing. <u>The Interpreters Bible</u> says the word used for music is also translated as a name for a specific wind instrument resembling the bagpipe.[25] Anyone who has ever been around an event where a bagpipe is played knows how well the sound of the instrument carries. In the cycle of the celebration, the guests eat first and then dance. That means the food is gone and the revelry has begun.

When the older son asks one of the slaves about the celebration we should experience the boiling of his blood. Tension rises here, for anger is the appropriate response. His brother, who does not exist any more, has had the nerve to come home. The father has thrown a party for this "dead" son. To make matters worse, he has not been invited to the celebration.

We so often see the elder son in a bad light, but his response to the events at hand is fitting. We can put ourselves in his position. Our sibling has done the unimaginable. We have been working on the property, and no one comes to let us know about the party. Then when we accidentally stumble onto the celebration we hear the music and dancing.

We can have that empathetic connection since many of us have found ourselves wronged. Maybe there was a party and we were not invited. Maybe a promotion at work was handled secretly so we were not able to apply for the position. It could be that we were counting on someone to support our views in a debate only to find he or she changed camps. This event is not just sad; it is wrong. In this "wrongness" he refuses to go into the party.

His father came out and began to plead with him. But he answered his father, "Listen! For all these years I have been working like a slave for you, and I have never disobeyed your command; yet you have never given me even a young goat so that I might celebrate with my friends. But when this son of yours came back, who has devoured your property with prostitutes, you killed the fatted calf for him!" (Luke 15: 28b-30 NRSV)

Realizing the crisis on the outside, the father leaves the party to come and personally invite the elder son to join the festivities. Here again the father breaks tradition. Wendt says, "The father should not leave his place of honor. He should stay inside with the guests! To go outside would again be demeaning."[26] But he dares to leave the guests and come face-to-face with his son. He may not have been prepared for the sudden outburst of anger. In this shame/honor society, a son does not chastise a parent. However, even in the surprising actions of the younger son, he always begins his conversation with respect. At the beginning of the parable, he says, "*Father*, give me my share . . . ." When he realizes his mistake, he rehearses with "I will say to him, '*Father*, I have sinned . . . .'" And upon the return he initiates his defense by declaring, "*Father*, I have sinned."

The elder son does not begin his response politely. "Listen!" This is the response of one tightly-coiled spring, just about to be released. Nothing is kind and gentle here. He is ready to attack, and even though he has not rehearsed his speech as did his brother, he has his thoughts in order.

He first establishes his place within the family by declaring that he has worked hard for years – as hard as a slave. He has never crossed his father or disobeyed his father's command to go, do, or fetch. Then he speaks of his lack of reward: his father has not given him a small goat to have a party with his friends, a party of nine to fifteen friends.

We notice that the older son does not call the younger son his brother. In his accusation to the father, which seems to have an element of finger-pointing, he addresses the sibling as "your son." The feeling rises, which tells us that even though the father has forgiven the younger son, the older son still considers him "dead."

Then we realize that news of the younger son's escapades has reached home. "Squander" has been replaced with the word "devoured." To squander implies a frivolous action, casting the cash he had received to the wind and having a grand time. However, to devour has the tone of a predator, moving with deliberate precision. One-third of the wealth of the family has been swallowed up.

The shock is what has devoured the cash – prostitutes. How did he know? Who told on the younger son? Was the father aware of this rumor? In response to this one who has devoured the wealth, what does the father do? Not what one would expect. He throws a party with the fatted calf, not just a party but a big party, already past the feast stage and moving to music and dancing. I can sense the rage, feel the heat of his anger, and empathize with him because I too have had the experience of being wronged.

Then the father said to him, "Son, you are always with me, and all that is mine is yours. But we had to celebrate and rejoice, because this brother of yours was dead and has come to life; he was lost and has been found." (Luke 15:31-32 NRSV)

The mood suddenly shifts to tenderness. The father addresses the elder son and reminds him of his position in the family when he says "son." The elder son has been faithful. Everything belongs to him, and that will not change. Even though the younger brother has been brought back into the household, the balance of the inheritance is not affected. "But," the father may have replied, "it is time to collect the pieces of the broken pot which divided this family." They celebrate because the family circle, which had been cracked, is now restored.

Then the parable ends. We want to cry out, "Wait! Tell us the rest of the story!" Does the older son yield to the words of the father? Does the elder son return to the field never to enter the party? Will there be reconciliation between the brothers? Boomershine says, "The final action of the parable is left in the hands of the elder son/listener."[27] Herein lies the power of a parable. We have the ability to finish the story. We write the end.

The power of this story lies in its ability to touch so many lives. It seems to find us wherever we are on life's road. We may find ourselves in that youthful rebellion. We may experience the parental element of the parable by identifying with the father. We have all felt as if we knew better how to handle our lives. We have all made mistakes. We have all had the occasion to admit our mistakes. We have all received forgiveness. And, most likely, we have all been angry - really angry - when we felt we were wronged.

Sharing the Text

The beginning of the chapter presented a method for reading and examining the text. This last section addresses the method of sharing the text with the listener.

When the community gathers for worship, there comes a time in the service when the Word is proclaimed. I have never been in a worship service where the proclaimer/preacher said, "Now, if everyone will turn to Luke 15, we will silently read the text before I begin my message for the day." No, we proclaim the Word of God aloud. Nothing sets the atmosphere for the sermon/proclamation any better than the effective presenting of the scripture text. I suggest two methods of textual presentation.

The first method is the memorizing of text. This works best with narrative texts. The stories of Jesus, the parables, the stories of Genesis and Exodus began as oral story, and it is not difficult to turn them back into oral story. In the section on examining the text, I suggested breaking the text into sections and voices using color. (One can simply insert blank spaces between the sections.) This provides a visual concept of the story structure.

A simple way of memorizing the text is to learn the story block-by-block. Once a small block of text is memorized, then we add the next block. By learning the smaller sections and stacking them together we will find the memorization process is not as difficult as we so often make it. I will say that memorization is a discipline and with practice the process is less time-consuming. We should not attempt to learn the story in its entirety in one session.

This is an oral event. When we work on the story we should do so in a place where we can read and learn the story by saying it aloud. I also suggest a place where we can learn the story on our feet. It helps me to be up and moving as I memorize the text. This also allows me to be more animated as I tell the story. Finally, we should not worry about being so precise with the memorization. When we struggle to get every word "right," the listener can sense an anxiety and tension. To tell the story is just that – tell the story. I am sure the apostles did not tell the stories of Jesus word-for-word as they happened. They told the stories from the heart. We should be accurate in the telling of the text so the people will accept the hearing as the Word of the Lord, but, on the other hand, we should tell it in our own voice, at our tempo, with our passion.

Thomas Boomershine's book <u>Story Journey: An Invitation to the Gospel as Storytelling</u> offers a methodology for storytelling in a religious setting. Boomershine, through the use of many biblical stories, offers both the pattern for learning the story along with how story can be used in ministry. Topics include Learning the Story Alone, Learning the Story with a Friend, Learning the Story as Story, and The Story in Preaching.

If, in the hectic life of a preacher/proclaimer/pastor, we do not have time to memorize the story or if the text is not narrative in nature, the next best thing is to read the text – and read it well. Again, we should use the format of breaking the story into segments, which allows for a visual clue to voicing and pacing.

Richard F. Ward wrote a small handbook for Discipleship Resources titled <u>Your Ministry of Reading Scripture Aloud</u>.[28] In his small book he offers direction on how to prepare for public reading in a chapter on "How Do I 'Get to Know' My Text?"

This chapter has illustrated methods for reading the text, examining the text, investigating forensically the text, and the sharing of the text. The previous chapter presented the elements which create the worship sensorium via the selecting a text, experiencing the text, bridging the text, imaging the text, and proclaiming the text. The next chapter will put into practice the elements in these two chapters as we create of a worship sensorium, including the setting of the service and the presentation of a sermon/proclamation on the text found in Luke 15.

Chapter 5 Endnotes

1. Barry Kiger, Lecture for the Birmingham-West District Bible Conference, 1996.
2. Jeremias, <u>The Parables of Jesus</u>, 129.
3. Page, <u>Jesus and the Land</u>, 106.
4. Jeremias, 129.
5. Kiger, 1996.
6. <u>Interpreter's Bible</u>, Volume 8, 272.
7. Boomershine, <u>Story Journey</u>, 79.
8. Talbert, <u>Reading Luke</u>, 149.
9. Scott, <u>Hear Then the Parable</u>, 114.
10. Scott.
11. This miracle story is found in Mark 5:1-17.
12. Wendt, <u>The Parables of Jesus</u>, 52.
13. <u>Interpreter's Bible</u>, 273.
14. <u>Dictionary of Biblical Imagery</u>, 665.
15. Page, 107.
16. Talbert, 150.

17. Scott, 117.
18. Talbert, 150.
19. <u>The New Interpreter's Bible</u>, Volume 9, 302.
20. Page, 107.
21. Jeremias, 130.
22. Tilley, <u>Story Theology</u>, 85.
23. Evelyn Laycock, Hewett United Methodist Church, 2002.
24. <u>Dictionary of Biblical Imagery</u>, 132.
25. <u>Interpreter's Bible</u>, 278.
26. Wendt, 55.
27. Boomershine, 73.
28. Ward, <u>Your Ministry of Reading Scripture Aloud</u>, Discipleship Resources, 1989.

CHAPTER 6
GOSPELTELLING IN PRAXIS

Moving from analytical to praxis, this chapter illustrates and puts into practice the concept of Gospeltelling. This chapter is not a definitive statement to say this is the way it must be created. Each worship setting is different. Every preacher/proclaimer has a different homiletical style. While some worship places are filled with access to technology, others continue to worship in a place where the only technology is a microphone. Creating of a local worship sensorium becomes a product of what is available.

In the Gospeltelling motif, the sermon/proclamation is not a singular event but rather a part of the entire worship sensorium. A sermon/proclamation based on the parable of the father and sons found in Luke 15 is presented in this chapter; therefore, the illustrations and suggestions which follow specifically address that particular text. If possible, everything involved in the gathering should center on the main theme/text. The sermon/proclamation itself must be included as an integral part of the sensorium. Stationary visual settings, music, multimedia, and a specific image to be used at the proclamation moment create the sensorium. What follows are the elements I would use to create the Gospeltelling sensorium for this text.

Stationary Visual Setting

Stationary visual settings, often called worship centers, can be set in the worship space or at the entry of that space. Sight is the first of our senses to be impacted as we enter the worship space. The sensory stage can be set by having those who enter the worship space immediately confront an image. A table near the entrance or in a prominent visual place inside the worship space itself can be used as the visual introduction of the theme/text. As in the Relational Bridge, we can use a mixture of both ancient and modern symbols to create an understanding.

Money is definitely a bridging symbol addressing the issue of asking for the inheritance. We might not feel comfortable placing "lose" money in a public place. A will, stocks, and/or bonds can also represent the inheritance. A map can be used to illustrate directions to a distant land. A party hat or whistle represents the son's extravagant living. To symbolize his falling we could use corn cobs or dirty clothes. Symbols of the homecoming could be a ring or shoes and a robe. The last section of the parable is difficult to portray in concrete symbols. How does one symbolize anger and a sense of unfairness? This attribute can better be illustrated through a different medium.

I would not attempt to tell the entire story via symbols, just use enough to create a connection. I have used symbols which recall the welcoming back into the family. The father calls for a robe, a ring, and shoes. The setting may not bring to mind the story upon the entrance to the worship/gathering, but it can be recalled during the service and the sermon/proclamation.

Music

Music is important element of the worship/gathering event. It involves sound, sight, and feeling. In a traditional service, with a denominational hymnal, hymns can be used to address a particular text or theme. In the <u>United Methodist Hymnal</u>, in the section "Index of Scripture," a suggestion of hymn number 343, *Come Back Quickly to the Lord*, written by Young Taik Chun, is listed for the Luke 15 text.[1]

For this particular parable, my first thought for traditional music sends me to an old hymn *Come, Ye Sinners, Poor and Needy*.[2] The tune I prefer, *Restoration*, has a haunting effect. Portions of the song are as follows:

> Come, ye sinners, poor and needy, weak and wounded, sick and sore;
> Jesus ready stands to save you, full of pity, love, and pow'r.
> *Let not conscience make you linger, nor of fitness fondly dream;*
> *All the fitness he requireth is to feel your need of him.*
> Come, ye weary, heavy laden, bruised and mangled by the fall,
> If you tarry till you're better, you will never come at all
> *I will arise and go to Jesus; he will embrace me in his arms;*
> *In the arms of my dear Savior, O there are ten thousand charms.*

The chorus lifts the refrain of the younger son: "I will arise and go to Jesus; he will embrace me in his arms." For me this paints the image of the father embracing the son upon his return. The tune may not be familiar, but it is simple enough that a gathered people can quickly join the singing.

A contemporary song which I also associate with lostness and reconciliation is *Mercy Came Running*, by Phillips, Craig, and Dean. Within the words of this song we find elements of security and safety, a loss of that security leading to despair, and finally the reconciliation:

Once there was a holy place; evidence of God's embrace.
And I can almost see mercy's face pressed against the veil.
Looking down with longing eyes, Mercy must have realized.
That once His blood was sacrificed freedom would prevail.

Once there was a broken heart. Way to human from the start.
And all the years left it torn apart, hopeless and afraid.
Walls I never meant to build left this prisoner unfulfilled.
Freedom called but even still it seemed so far away

Sometimes I still feel so far. So far from where I really should be.
He gently calls to my heart just to remind me

Chorus: *Mercy came running, like a prisoner set free.*
Past all my failures to the point of my need
When the sin that I carried was all I could see.
And when I could not reach mercy, Mercy came running to me[3]

Once, while working with this text, I decided to write a song based on the prodigal son's story:

COME, CELEBRATE WITH ME

He came asking for his part – and left home for a new start
    But he wasted all, was left penniless, alone.
Hard times fell upon that land, no one there gave him a hand,
    Victim of those shallow friends, without a home.

In desperation he went down to the farm outside town,
    Who sent him out to feed the pigs alone.
In shame and hunger his heart bled, on his knees the swine he fed,
    Would he dare to taste those pods of which they eat?

In the mire where he lay, remembered on that day
    How his father's slaves had bread enough and more.

> Standing up he lifts his head, "I now go to see my dad!"
>   And he traveled down the road from whence he came.
>
> From a distance the father spied a young man coming in full stride
>   He saw the fear and pain within his look.
> With open arms he brought him back, a robe and shoes, the fatted calf.
>   Forgiven there the boy received a brand new start.
>
> ***chorus***
> Come, celebrate with me, the one who died now lives you see.
> Though he was lost, now he's back – so I say to thee,
> Come, celebrate with me.
>
> When in the pit a light had shown
> No matter the miles you walk you're never far from home.[4]

Many songs address the themes of pride, lostness, and reconciliation. The idea is to enfold the entire worship service with the themes from the parable. If possible, we should let every song, vocal and instrumental, illustrate the attributes of the parable or theme of the worship event.

Multimedia Elements

At the very beginning of this section, I strongly suggest that a church, congregation, or gathered community purchase a copyright license, which gives the participating group permission to use music and video resource legally.

The resources for multimedia segments are many. Also many groups have already isolated media clips associated with a particular text. One such Internet site which offers suggestions is *The Text This Week*. Under the tab for movie index, several clips are suggested, including a segment from *Wizard of Oz*, in which "Dorothy leaves home, wanders, and returns with new appreciation for those who love her." From the film *Boiler Room*, a clip tells how "Seth strays from his father's values. His father remains loyal to him at great cost to himself. Seth turns in the company and returns to his father's value system."[5]

The American Bible Society produced a short music video titled *A Father and Two Sons*.[6]   This production, with Dr. Thomas Boomershine as chief consultant, is a video retelling of the Luke 15 parable using a western motif. A female "country" singer becomes the narrator, and the main characters work on a Western ranch. It is a passionate retelling, illustrating the varied dynamics of the story. Images portray inclusiveness of differing age, gender, and race, which invite all to become a part of the story. Even though the clip has a country music effect, the words of the song track the text with amazing accuracy.

Another video clip for use in connection with the prodigal son text is from the fairytale by Rob Reiner titled *The Princess Bride*.[7] In Chapter 21 on the DVD, the hero has had the life sucked out of him by the villain and has been taken deep into the forest to the home of Miracle Max in hopes that Max can bring the hero back to life. In the segment, Miracle Max examines the hero and declares that they are in luck: the man is only "mostly dead" and not "all-the-way dead," which is worse. To be "mostly dead" means there is a possibility that he can be brought back to life. It is a segment filled with humor and is suitable viewing for anyone. In the parable, the son is "mostly dead" not "completely dead." He is revived by the reception of his father.

Imaging the Text

Imaging the text is the selection process by which an image or images are selected to address the text/theme. We can easily develop a series of images which address each section of the Luke 15 parable. A parent and child in conflict, a person leaving home, someone down and out are possible images. To finish the parable, we see images of the embracing father and son, the celebration gathering, and the father and older son in a heated discussion.

Ordinarily, I try to choose a single image to address the issue or point made by the story/parable. This particular parable is long with scene changes. We experience in the parable the son confronting the father, the younger son leaving home of the younger son, his wasting the inheritance, his despair, his awakening, his return, the father's compassion and reinstatement of the son, the celebration, and the confrontation with the older son. With such a complex story, I have used images which address each section of the parable.

Several years ago I told the Luke 15 parable to a worshiping group of men. Unknown to me, one of the participants was the artist-in-residence at a local school. Not long after my telling the story, he gave me a drawing that he had created in response to the telling. I have used this image because it has such a powerful connection to me and the story.

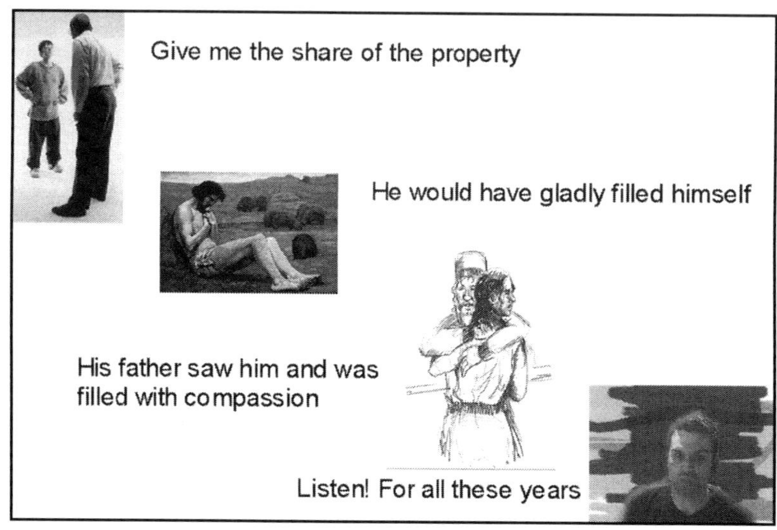

All of these components assist in the creation of a sensorium of sight, sound, and emotional connection. The only thing lacking is the sense of smell, and I do not think we would want the smell of pigs at a worship gathering. And the smell of barbecued meat would distract as those in attendance would spend the time gazing at their watches, waiting to rush out to their next meal.

Worship is not a singular event. It must be multifaceted, and it must also create the bridge we travel between the ancient text and the modern world. Again, this is not intended to be an all-inclusive illustration of the worship/gathering event but rather to address those elements which directly impact and connect to the proclamation moment. In a team approach to worship, whether that team is a complex union of specialists or the cross-the-table discussion between pastor and church music director, the object is to make the entire worship/gathering event congruent.

The Gospeltelling Proclamation

In this section I take some literary and grammatical liberties. This is intended to be an oral event, and often the boundaries of correct written text are not congruent with an oral pattern. Bold and capitalized characters offer a visual sense of verbal action. There are times in oral production when we can get away with a sentence fragment and run-on phrasing. As we read this section, we do so with an oral/aural approach. I also insert the images I would use for the sermon. The photographs used, to the best of my knowledge and my ability to research their origins, are public domain images.

When You Realize You've Made A Mistake
A Gospeltelling Moment from Luke 15:11-32

"I will arise and go to Jesus, he will embrace me in his arms ..."

Once upon a time there was a high-ranking executive, who was filled with hope and promise. He listened to the wrong people and took advantage of his powerful position at the expense of others. His poor decisions led to his company being penalized. When the exec was removed from his position and asked to pay restitution for the loss, he began a fierce legal battle. Finally, the Board of Directors agreed that if the man would simply admit publicly to what he had done they would forgive the debt and reinstate him to his previous position. But he was a stubborn individual and refused to admit to the wrongdoing. He lost his job because he would not admit to making a mistake.

We live in a society today which accepts no personal blame. If you are hyperactive, it is because of something your mother ate while she was carrying you in the womb. If you are violent it is because your parents spanked you. I am amazed at the continual suing of the tobacco companies by those who have cancer. A warning label was placed on tobacco products in 1965! For **forty years** people have heard the cry – DON'T SMOKE! But they continue - and then blame the tobacco company.

The same scenario was recently played out by someone who sued McDonald's restaurant because the food is *addictive* and makes people obese. HELLO!!

The Moral Fiber of our society is weak. We now freely use language that was once thought to be used only on the docks and in men's locker rooms. We watch movies whose content in a past time could be seen only in secured theaters. We excuse every wrong by blaming someone else. But there will come a time when we must answer for our decisions. When we come face-to-face with Jesus – who will you blame?

Charles Page is an archaeologist, who has spent years researching the culture of the people living in the area we call the Holy Land. He tells of a dinner party he attended in Israel. Being a scholar of Middle Eastern culture, he wanted to watch the response of the men who had gathered for the evening.

"Let me tell you a story. There is a man who has two sons. The younger son comes to the father one day and say, 'Dad, I want my part of the inheritance - now!'"

"Stop!" the men said in almost a shouting tone. "You can tell us another story!"

"No," said Charles, "I want to finish this one."

"NO!" the men continued. "We do not want to hear this story."

"Why?"

"Because it would never happen."

"But let's just imagine that it did," Charles continued.

"No. This would never happen in a Jewish family."

When Jesus began this parable, shock streaked across the souls of the listeners like summer lightning. One does not ask about the inheritance before the **"right time,"** and as long as the father is still alive, there will never be a **"right time."**

If the son dares to demand, "Give Me," the implication is that he is telling his father "I wish you were dead." I've been mad at my father. And I have been REALLY MAD – but not to the point of telling my father "I wish you were dead!" And I have been angry with my children – but never **that** mad!!

To the absolute astonishment of those with Jesus – he makes the scene even darker. Jesus makes the moment a two-sided event when the father <u>agrees</u> to give the son his portion of the inheritance. In doing so, the father then declares to the son, and to the community, that from that point on it would be as if the son never existed or, at best, has died. Suddenly, we have both declaring each other dead.

In a society where HONOR is primary – this is an unbelievable act. The event leads to an action called the *KeZaZah* – the breaking of the pot. And with that *crash* the family is shattered – broken – incomplete – all because the son asked the question at the wrong time.

I read a story about a pastor in Iran who had one of his parishioners enter his office in a panic. "My son wants me to die!" "Why?" "My son brought up the subject of the inheritance." As in the ancient story Jesus tells, that subject meant the son was looking for the father to die. Three months later the man – who up until that time was in good health – suddenly died. When the pastor arrived at the man's home, he approached the wife to offer his sympathy. In that intimate moment of sorrow, the wife said, "He really died the night his son asked about the inheritance."

The Law was very specific about the division of the inheritance. The older son always gets a double portion. With two sons, the older son receives two-thirds of the estate and the younger son one-third. The estate is comprised of both real and liquid assets. It appears the father gives the younger son his inheritance in tangible goods – money, jewelry, pots and pans! Then the proud son cashes in the inheritance and, with his pockets full of money, heads toward the bright lights – the Big City – GENTILE COUNTRY!

Can't fault him for that! How many of us have turned a deaf ear to our parents? And when they would ask us to simply listen – we would plug our ears and shut down our minds. How many of us, in our teens, thought our parents were out of touch with the world? Detached from reality? <u>Just plain dumb!</u>? Samuel Clemons, also known as Mark Twain, once wrote: "When I was a boy of fourteen, my father was so ignorant I could hardly stand to have the old man around. But when I got to be twenty-one, I was astonished at how much the old man had learned in seven years."

Most have engaged in the mental warfare as, when we are being chastised by our parent, or coach, or best friend for our lack of understanding, we stand there in the silence of our mental rebuttal, quietly whispering to our soul, "They just don't understand!"

He may have plans to invest and make it rich! Maybe even start a business in a big city. Then he will show them who knows best! "I will return home rich and important."

He wanders off toward the distant land and begins his new life. Entering a promising village, maybe he decides to "buy" some new, influential friends. So the party begins! He may think he has enough money to last him a lifetime. He will spend some money buying his position and then use the rest to build his empire. It is only a dream.

We are not privy to the events in the distant land, but whatever happened, we **are** told by Jesus, as he continues the story, he ***"squandered his wealth."***

AND WHEN ALL WAS GONE – ALL WAS GONE: money, friends, opportunity. And when he thought he was at his lowest point – **things got worse.** Famine!

I have been in those places. Maybe you have been there too. Where you had to look up to see bottom. Where you would do almost anything just to keep going. He is desperate. He was starving. <u>He</u> – <u>is</u> –<u>alone</u>!

In this foreign land – this distant country – in this pagan society, he has to do something. So he hires himself out to a local farmer. **Hires himself!** Slaves in this society had rights – places to sleep, food to eat, security. But the hired hand, one who went seeking or begging – was lower than a slave – no benefits, no security, no respect.

The listeners sensed, maybe from the tone of Jesus' voice, that the younger son had no dignity left. He is in a state of utter despair and hopelessness.

Alone – desperate – hungry, the prodigal is sent to herd pigs. Have you ever been around pigs? They are not cute little pink animals. They are big, noisy, stinky, and sometimes vicious animals. And they were not kept in muddy pens but were herded like sheep. I am sure the smell and the incessant grunting are driving the son deeper into a pit of despair. I have imagined that, while he is running around, trying to keep control of the swine, he holds out a hand to those passing by who turn a blind eye: "Why would we want to give **this foreigner** anything?" Then comes one of the most powerful statements in this parable: **"And No One Gave Him Anything."** *There is no deeper sense of loneliness.*

A Jewish Proverb says: "When an Israelite reaches a place that he will eat carob beans, then he will return to God." What are carob beans? Pig Food!! He reaches a place where he desires to eat pig food!

Suddenly The Light Comes ON!! *"But when he came to himself ..."* One translation says: *"But when he was in his right mind"*– when the light comes on, when the clouds begin to break, when the ice of his despair begins to melt - his thinking becomes clear. **"What I Need To Do Is GO HOME!"**

He rehearses his speech – "Father, I have sinned against heaven and before you; I am no longer worth to be called your son; treat me like one of your hired hands." He thinks, "I have sinned against heaven - by declaring my father dead. And against my father by wasting the inheritance." And so he returned – not to be a son but rather a servant, a hired hand.

And so he gets up – and goes home. And while he is still a Great Distance away, his father sees him – and is filled with compassion. I hear the father as he sees his son who is dirty, gaunt, and struggling, say, *"Oh, son!"* And he runs to him.

In this society, men of honor did not run. The slaves wore short robes to work in. Men of Honor wore long robes – not designed for anything but regalness and respect. But he drops all the baggage of cultural norm and **RUNS** to his son.

Why was he running? Our first thought is that he has missed his son and is ready for the reunion. But it is deeper. When the son declares his *father dead*, he brings dishonor on the family and the community. It would be within the rights of the community once they spot the prodigal, to attack or even stone him to death to restore honor. THE FATHER WAS RUNNING TO PROTECT SON. He reaches him and embraces him. Shrouding him in his own robe - - protecting him from the potential threat. It is a powerful moment of reconciliation.

Have you ever been estranged? Something happens and suddenly a person or a friend stops speaking to you. You may not know why. You replay history in your mind hoping to discover what happened. **THEN suddenly you meet** – maybe by accident or by force. In that moment both of you realize the pain caused by the impenetrable wall – and you move toward each other – maybe not in an embrace but in spiritual renewal – reunion!

The Father never asks any questions and even stops the son's speech before he can make his plea. He orders the servants to bring the best robe – and don't just bring the best robe - you, the slave, must put it on this wayward son. It is a symbol of reconciliation, of acceptance, of once again being a part of the family.

He then instructs the slaves to put a ring on the son's hand – a signet ring symbolizing his authority. And tells the slaves –*the slaves* – to put shoes on his son's feet. Only slaves went around barefoot. He is not being received as a slave or hired servant – he is being received as a son. And the slaves – those who knew the son before, who heard about the rip in the family's fabric, who may have been told the rumors of his deeds in the distant land – are now having to place the robe, the ring, and the shoes on the son's feet for he ow can tell them what to do and where to go.

Then the father declares -**KILL THE FATTED CALF AND LET'S PARTY!!** *"For this, son of mine was **dead** and is alive again, he was **lost** and is found."* The pottery has been repaired – the family circle is now complete. It's time to celebrate!

This would be such a nice place to end the story. The wayward, prodigal son returns and is welcomed back into the family – the party is joyful and the community accepts his apology. But this is NOT the end of the story.

We shift suddenly to the other brother – the faithful son. He has been working hard out in the fields and comes home to a big surprise! **A party is going on!!** And the band is playing and people are dancing! **What's Going On?!**

The older son catches a servant and asks about the party. The servant replies, "You mean you don't know? Your brother has returned and your father has killed the fatted calf and had this party because your brother has come home safe and sound."

WHAT!!! - You can begin to see the older son's face turning red, his eyes glazed and fixed, the hair on the back of his neck standing straight up. This guy is not just mad - **he is Angry!!** Angry at the throwing of a party for the rebellious son who told Dad, "I wish you were dead!" Angry at the fact that his father so grandly welcomed him home! Angry that a party has been thrown and he was not even invited!

Since the older son is now officially the owner of all things on the homestead, it is his responsibility to be the host at the party. But was he even asked? NO!!!

And what is worse, when the older son hears the music and dancing he knows the feast is over – the food gone. All of this adds insult to injury. Like pouring salt into an open wound.

He has every right to be angry. But reality crashes in when we realize that *Life* does not always play by the rules. *Life* is not always predictable. *LIFE* IS NOT ALWAYS FAIR.

When he refuses to go inside to the party, the father comes out to talk to the older son - to invite this *faithful* son to a party thrown for his "dead brother."

Still fuming, he attacks his father with both barrels – **"LISTEN!!** FOR ALL these years I have been **working like a slave** for you, and I have **never** disobeyed your command. You have **never even given me a young goat** to have a party with my friends. – *BUT* – when this -**your son** – comes home, who has wasted the inheritance on prostitutes – you kill the fatted calf and throw a big party!

The father never loses his cool. Maybe he realizes that the older son's feelings are indeed legitimate. But then he reminds the older son of his position, "Son, you are always with me and everything – and I mean *everything* –is yours. And nothing is going to change when it comes to the inheritance. But we need to celebrate – **WE** need to celebrate because your brother is now home. He was dead and has come to life! He was lost and has been found!"

I love the movie *Princess Bride* – the fairytale story of the beautiful princes, handsome hero, and the dastardly villain. In the movie the hero has been captured by the villain and placed in his torture machine which can literally suck the life out of a person. After the pain and horror of the machine does its work, the hero is left for dead. But – as fairytales go – the friends of the hero come and take his limp and lifeless body deep into the woods to the house of Miracle Max. They ask Miracle Max for a miracle – bring the hero back to life. Max examines the hero and finally declares, "You're in luck. He is only mostly dead." "Mostly dead?" they say. "Yes," replies Max. "If he were all the way dead there would be nothing I could do. But, since he is only mostly dead – well – there's hope."

The son is only mostly dead – grace revives him. *He's Back*!

Harold Kushner, a Jewish Rabbi, wrote a book several years ago titled <u>When All You Ever Wanted Isn't Enough</u>. We all have a grand dream of what we wish life will give us. Maybe you want a large salary or power over the masses. Or maybe you want a big house, or a fast car, or lots of friends. There is that old saying: "Be careful what you pray for – you may get it – and it may not be what you expected!"

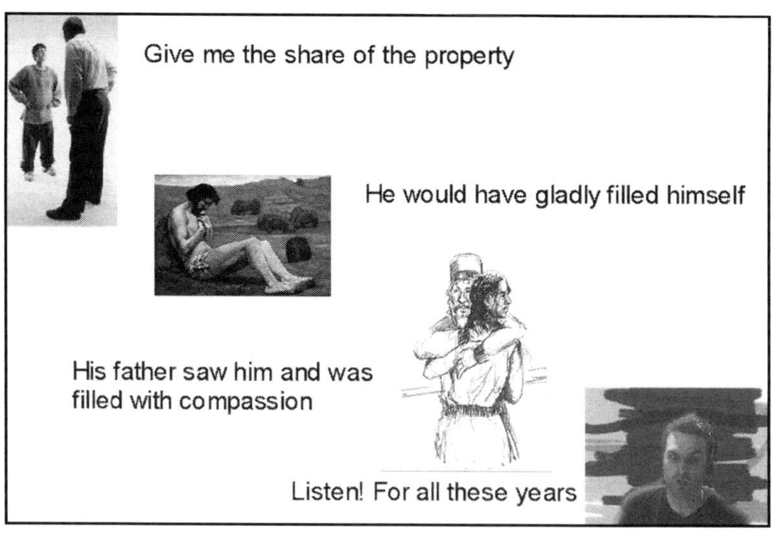

What mistakes have you made that cost you something valuable? What mistakes have you made that cost others? The younger son loses it all: money, friends, family – but admits he is wrong – then goes back home.

When you realize you have made a mistake – admit your mistake, try to make things right, and then, move on.

Jesus calls us to be active – not to stop and spend the rest of our lives wallowing with the pigs. When we reach a place where we realize our mistakes, we too need to be willing to sing the song: *I will arise and go to Jesus.*

AMEN

Chapter 6 Endnotes

1. <u>The United Methodist Hymnal</u>, 925.
2. Joseph Hart, *Come, Ye Sinners, Poor and Needy*, 1759.
3. Phillips, Craig, and Dean, *Favorite Songs of All, Mercy Came Running,* Star Song Records, 1998.
4. D. Jonathan Watts, *Come Celebrate With Me*, 1992.
5. The Text Week, http://www.textweek.com/movies/prodigal.htm.
6. *A Father and Two Sons*, American Bible Society, 1995.
7. Rob Reiner, dir., *The Princess Bride*, MGM Home Entertainment, 2001.

CHAPTER 7
THE GOSPELTELLING "SO WHAT"

In Dr. Craddock's class on preaching, he challenged us to look back on the sermon we had prepared and ask the question "So What?" Will it make any difference to those who are listening? Will it make any difference in my life? Is it really what God wants to say – now? So it is, as I glance backward that I too must ask that question about this work – "So What?"

In Chapter 1, I discovered that worship – ever changing – ever constant – continues to be the anchor for the community of faith. It has, throughout the generations, shifted and moved and realigned itself to be relational to the community and steadfast in its faith. Worship must continue to embrace the generation interpreting its message according to their paradigm – not a past standard. Worship, when done with integrity, sincerity, and faith, can continue to attract those whose spirit is drawn to the Spirit through new and vibrant avenues. The Church of Digital Culture with its energy, its creativity, its daring to stretch the boundaries of worship, can boldly say, "We can make a difference!" in response to the "So What?" question.

In Chapter 2, I observed that the church – ever changing – ever dividing, yet ever singular in purpose – still seeks to hear the Word. At every branching of the Church Tree, a person of passion and vision cried out with a new voice. The voice has changed from a fireside story to a table-side apologetic. It has moved from shrouded mystery to blue-sky clarity. The proclamation has made an exit from dark, candle-lighted halls to brilliant, larger-than-life images on expanding screens. As the prophets cried, "Thus says the Lord!" and, as Jesus declared, "You with ears, listen," today we look back over the long road of history and stretch towards the future with the words, "Go and do likewise." Today the Digital Culture faces many ethical, political, and theological issues. If those who proclaim the Word with a passion strive to redirect an erring thought or blow the fog away from dimming standards so the Light of Christ can shine ever brighter, then we can address the "So What?" with a bold "Hear the Word of the Lord!"

In Chapter 3, I offered an exposure to the differing voices of the proclaimer. The voice of those who create deliberate patterns of thought and progression. The voice who weaves the Gospel in story narrative. I have lifted up the voice of past pain and current struggle in its blackness and the voice of a tender, nurturing woman in its gentleness. God does not discriminate when it comes to proclaiming the Word. God only seeks those with a passion and then allows those persons to lift high the cross in the voice God has given them. The variety of voice, the variation of tone, and the diversity of approach allows us to answer the "So What?" by saying "my voice made a difference."

In Chapter 4, I noted that we do not live in the past, we do not proclaim an outdated creed but a living, current, relevant faith. As much as many of us love nostalgia, we live in the present context, which, through God's ever expanding gift of imagination, communicates in a multisensory environment. Stained glass windows are replaced with PowerPoint slides. Long, wooden pews are replaced with folding chairs. The drown of the deep pitches of the pipe organ has been exchanged with the vibration of the guitar, the pulsating beat of the drum, and the clapping of hands. The reverent, soul-searching hymns have become joyful noises of praise. The pulpit, once shrouding the messenger, has disappeared as the proclaimer stands exposed before the people. I set forth the illustration of the Relational Bridge that connects the ancient text with digital culture concepts. I presented a methodology for the bringing that ancient text forward through the avenues of selecting, experiencing, bridging, imaging, and proclaiming the text.

I do not advocate a particular style or pattern of worship or homiletical construct. Variety is a gift from God. Jesus knew the power of variety – just look at who he chose as disciples! But the Word remains steadfast, and even in the extremes of holy places, there comes a response to the "So What," lifted from a Spirit-touched heart, "The word of God for the People of God!"

In Chapter 5, I presented a methodology for the forensic reconstruction of a story. This exegetical process of text discovery, based on the parable of the father and sons in Luke 15, addresses the elements of reading the text, examining the text, forensically investigating the text, and sharing the text. The methodical preparation of the text sets the stage for the proclamation itself. Again, I do not endorse a particular homiletical style. Each person, being unique, brings individual talents to the table and offers God's Word, using those talents. The "So What" in this chapter points to the *eureka* event - "Now I know what God wants me to say!"

Chapter 6 is a reflection of my own forensic experience with the Luke 15 text. I presented suggestions for the setting to lend nurture to the proclamation event. Through the pouring out of one's soul in the exposed moment of proclamation/preaching, the "So What" says "Amen."

And so I have searched my soul for the passion which Tom Boomershine challenged me to find. The driving force for what I do. The ever-tugging line between my soul and God. I find that passion in the proclamation of the Word of God. The opportunity to preach/proclaim drives me forwards in a vocation which requires me to stand before others – not to be lifted up, but as one who joins them on the journey. With that passion comes the desire to tell the truth, to make it relevant, and together – as a gathered community – to experience the presence of God. To proclaim the Gospel to a culture comfortable with computer technology and digital imagery is a challenge. To stand before a gathered community and share from the Bible and my life, at times, can be threatening. But that is the difference between a vocation and a calling. A calling is the soul-felt tug which says this is what God wants me to do. So, I have to personally answer the question "So What?" And in response I pray that, as I have attempted to bridge the ancient story to the contemporary setting, to someone – at least one – I have made a difference through Gospeltelling to a Digital Culture.

References

The Book of Discipline of the United Methodist Church. Nashville: The United Methodist Publishing House, 2004.

Boomershine, Thomas E. Story Journey: An Invitation to the Gospel as Storytelling. Nashville: Abingdon Press, 1988.

Craddock, Fred B. As One Without Authority. Nashville: Abingdon Press, 1979.

Craddock, Fred B. Overhearing the Gospel: Preaching and Teaching the Faith to Persons Who Have Heard It All Before. Nashville: Abingdon Press, 1978.

Craddock, Fred B. Preaching. Nashville: Abingdon Press, 1985.

Crossan, John Dominic and Jonathan L. Reed. Excavating Jesus: Beneath the Stones, Behind the Texts. New York: HarperCollins Publishers, 2001.

Edwards, O.C. A History of Preaching, Nashville: Abingdon Press, 2004.

Eslinger, Richard L. A New Hearing: Living Options in Homiletic Method. Nashville: Abingdon Press, 1987.

Gonzalez, Justo L. The Story of Christianity Volume 1: The Early Church to the Dawn of the Reformation. New York: Harper and Row, Publishers, 1984.

Gonzalez, Justo L. The Story of Christianity Volume 2: The Reformation to the Present Day. New York: Harper and Row, Publishers, 1985.

Hanson, K.C. and Douglas Oakman. Palestine in the Time of Jesus: Social Structures and Social Conflicts. Minneapolis: Fortress Press, 1998.

The Holy Bible: Contemporary English Version. New York: American Bible Society, 1995.

The Interpreter's Bible: A Commentary in Twelve Volumes. Nashville: Abingdon Press, 1952.

Jeremias, Joachim, The Parables of Jesus. New York: Charles Scribner's Sons, 1972.

Johnson, James Weldon. God's Trombones: Seven Negro Sermons in Verse. New York: The Viking Press, 1927.

Jones, Cheslyn, Geoffrey Wainwright, and Edward Yarnold, eds. The Study of the Liturgy. New York: Oxford University Press, 1978.

Kimball, Dan. Emerging Worship: Creating Worship Gathering for
     New Generations. Grand Rapids: emergentYS Books, 2004.
Lowry, Eugene L. Doing Time in the Pulpit: The Relationship
     Between Narrative and Preaching. Nashville: Abingdon Press,
     1985.
Metzger, Bruce M. The New Testament: Its Background, Growth,
     and Content. Nashville: Abingdon Press, 2003.
Metzger, Bruce M. and Michael D. Coogan, eds. The Oxford
     Companion to the Bible. New York: Oxford University Press,
     1993.
Metzger, Bruce M. and Roland E. Murphy. The New Oxford
     Annotated Bible: New Revised Standard Version. New York:
     Oxford University Press, 1991.
Mitchell, Henry H. Black Preaching. New York: Harper and Row,
     Publishers, 1979.
Morgan, John H., ed. J.W.C. Wand, The Greek and Latin Doctors.
     Bristol, Indiana: Wyndham Hall Press, 1990.
The New Interpreter's Bible: A Commentary in Twelve Volumes.
     Nashville: Abingdon Press, 1995.
Ong, Walter J. The Presence of the Word: Some Prolegomena for
     Cultural and Religious History. Minneapolis: University of
     Minnesota Press, 1967.
Ong, Walter J. Orality and Literacy: The Technologizing of the
     Word. New York: Methuen, 1982.
Page, Charles R. Jesus and the Land. Nashville: Abingdon Press,
     1995.
Pilch, John J. The Cultural Dictionary of the Bible. Collegeville,
     Minnesota: The Liturgical Press, 1999.
Procter, Samuel D. "How Shall They Hear?": Effective Preaching for
     Vital Faith. Valley Forge, Pennsylvania: Judson Press, 1992.
Ryken, Leland, James C. Wilhoit, and Tremper Longman, eds.
     Dictionary of Biblical Imagery. Downers Grove, Illinois:
     InterVarsity Press,1998.
Sample, Tex. Ministry in an Oral Culture: Living with Will Rogers,
     Uncle Remus, and Minnie Pearl. Louisville, Kentucky:
     Westminster/John Knox Press, 1994.
Sample, Tex. The Spectacle of Worship in a Wired World: Electronic
     Culture and the Gathered People of God. Nashville: Abingdon
     Press, 1998.

Scott, Brandon Scott. <u>Hear Then the Parable: A Commentary on the Parables of Jesus</u>. Minneapolis: Fortress Press, 1989.

Slaughter, Michael. <u>Out On The Edge: A Wake-up Call for Church Leaders on the Edge of the Media Reformation</u>. Nashville: Abingdon Press, 1998.

Spangenberg, August Gottlieb. <u>The Life of Nicholas Lewis Count Zinzendorf</u>. London: Samuel Holdsworth, 1838.

Sweet, Leonard I. <u>Quantum Spirituality: A Postmodern Apologetic</u>. Dayton, Ohio: Whaleprints, 1991.

Sweet, Leonard I., ed. <u>The Church in Emerging Culture: Five Perspectives</u>. Grand Rapids: emergentYS Books, 2003.

Talbert, Charles H. <u>Reading Luke: A Literary and Theological Commentary on the Third Gospel</u>. New York: Crossroad, 1989.

Tilley, Terrence W. <u>Story Theology</u>. Collegeville, Minnesota: The Liturgical Press, 1990.

Troeger, Thomas H. <u>Imagining A Sermon</u>. Nashville: Abingdon Press, 1990.

<u>The United Methodist Hymnal: Book of United Methodist Worship</u>. Nashville: The United Methodist Publishing House, 1989.

Ward, Richard F. <u>Your Ministry of Reading Scripture Aloud</u>. Nashville: Discipleship Resources, 1989.

Watts, D. Jonathan. <u>Genesis to Jesus to You: A Story Journey for Christian Education</u>. United Theological Seminary, 1994.

Wendt, H.N. <u>The Parables of Jesus</u>. Minneapolis: Crossways International, 1997.

Wilson, Len and Jason Moore. <u>Digital Storytellers: The Art of Communicating the Gospel in Worship</u>. Nashville: Abingdon Press, 2002.

Wilson-Kastner, Patricia. <u>Imagery for Preaching</u>. Minneapolis: Fortress Press, 1989.

About the Author

D. Jonathan Watts, Ph.D., teaches Religion, Philosophy, and Speech at Snead State Community College, Boaz, Alabama, and is an Elder in the North Alabama Conference of the United Methodist Church. Watts holds a Bachelor of Arts in Theology, a Master of Divinity degree, a Doctor of Ministry degree, and a Doctor of Philosophy degree which he received from the Graduate Theological Foundation upon successfully defending his dissertation in Oxford, England, where he studied at Christ Church College, Oxford University.

Jonathan has a broad background in church work as a lay person, a minister of music, and has twenty years in pastoral ministry. He and his wife Karen are active in the First United Methodist Church, Guntersville, Alabama. They have two daughters Lindsey and Whitney. He has conducted numerous workshops and retreats focusing on storytelling and preaching.